The Trivialization of God

THE TRIVIALIZATION OF GOD

THE DANGEROUS ILLUSION OF A MANAGEABLE DEITY

DONALD W. McCULLOUGH

NAVPRESS

BRINGING TRUTH TO LIFE

NavPress Publishing Group

P.O. Box 35001, Colorado Springs, Colorado 80935

Some of the anecdotal illustrations in this book are true to life
and are included with the permission of the persons involved. All
other illustrations are composites of real situations, and any
resemblance to people living or dead is coincidental.

Portions of chapters six and ten appeared in an earlier form in
Donald McCullough, "Holy God, Holy Church," *Incarnational
Ministry: The Presence of Christ in Church, Society, and Family—
Essays in Honor of Ray S. Anderson,* ed. Christian D. Kettler and
Todd H. Speidell (Colorado Springs: Helmers & Howard, 1990),
pp. 16-31.

Unless otherwise identified, all Scripture quotations in this publication are taken from the *New Revised Standard Version* (NRSV),
copyright 1989, by the Division of Christian Education of the
National Council of the Churches of Christ in the USA, used by
permission, all rights reserved.

McCullough, Donald W., 1949-
      The trivialization of God : the dangerous illusion of a
  manageable deity / Donald W. McCullough.
          p.   cm.
      Includes bibliographical references and indexes.
      ISBN 0-89109-909-3 (hardcover)
      1. God. 2. Holy, The. 3. Revelation. 4. Word of God
  (Theology) 5. Christian life. I. Title.
  BT102.M395 1995
  231—dc20   95-14409
                                                        CIP
Printed in the United States of America

1 2 3 4 5 6 7 8 9 10 11 12 13 14 15 16 17 18 19/99 98 97 96 95

FOR A FREE CATALOG OF
NAVPRESS BOOKS & BIBLE STUDIES,
CALL 1-800-366-7788 (USA)
or 1-416-499-4615 (CANADA)

To
the memory of
Alan E. Lewis
(1944–1994)

Contents

Acknowledgments

I began this book while serving as pastor of Solana Beach Presbyterian Church, a ministry I enjoyed for nearly fourteen years. This remarkable congregation of God's people graced my life in many ways: they shared joys and sorrows, trusted my leadership, affirmed my gifts, tolerated my weaknesses, supported my family, and helped me become a better disciple of Jesus Christ. I love them deeply, and I miss them greatly.

Halfway through the manuscript I accepted the invitation to become President of San Francisco Theological Seminary. It was not an easy decision, but I sensed God's call and thus started a new adventure in ministry. My new colleagues have embraced me with warm hospitality, and I look forward to many years of partnership in the great task of training future leaders for the church.

Learning to lead an educational institution was not the most propitious time for finishing a book, but with God's gracious help the last words were finally set to paper and sent to a very patient publisher. NavPress believed in this project from the beginning and has been encouraging through the long months of writing.

Kathy Yanni was a wonderful editor, an author's dream. She knew when to criticize and when to affirm, when to hold her ground and when to concede. Her wit and wisdom, her partnership and friendship, have made this a much better book.

Susie Dysland provided outstanding secretarial assistance during my last four-and-a-half years in Solana Beach; her faithful efficiency organized my life in ways that made possible the writing of a book. And Betty Waggoner, here at SFTS, has cheerfully and capably taken up the challenge, particularly in helping to orient me in the social dynamics of my new role.

The first chapter was written amid the beautiful maple trees of New Hampshire at the home of Jerry and Patti Filiciotto. The ninth was written in the home of Art Jensen, fortified by a daily rationing of his famous oatmeal cookies. I'm grateful for the generosity of these friends.

My wife, Karen, and my daughters, Jennifer and Joy, have been loving and supportive not only through the travails of creating a book, but also during this time of transition in our family life. Their many gifts to me are more than I deserve.

Many of the ideas in this book (particularly my understanding of the holiness of God) germinated during doctoral studies at the University of Edinburgh. The supervisor of my thesis was the Rev. Dr. Alan E. Lewis. He was uncompromising in his demand for excellence in research, but through the intellectual give and take a relationship formed that grew into a bond of cherished friendship. He had a brilliant mind and a humble spirit, a passionate faith and a gentle manner. I now miss our conversations about theology and politics and novels; I miss his encouragement and ready laughter; I miss hearing him say in his lilting brogue, "Love to your family; God bless. . . ." His untimely death has left a painful hole in my life. In one of our last conversations, as he lay on a bed of suffering, I told him I would dedicate my next book to him. He seemed embarrassed, but also, I think, a little pleased.

Who would fashion a god or cast an image
that can do no good?
ISAIAH 44:10

To whom then will you compare me,
or who is my equal? says the Holy One.
ISAIAH 40:25

CHAPTER ONE

The Trivialization
of God

Visit a church on Sunday morning—almost any will do—and you will likely find a congregation comfortably relating to a deity who fits nicely within precise doctrinal positions, or who lends almighty support to social crusades, or who conforms to individual spiritual experiences. But you will not likely find much awe or sense of mystery. The only sweaty palms will be those of the preacher unsure whether the sermon will go over; the only shaking knees will be those of the soloist about to sing the offertory.

The New Testament warns us, "offer to God an acceptable worship with reverence and awe; for indeed our God is a consuming fire" (Hebrews 12:28-29). But reverence and awe have often been replaced by a yawn of familiarity. The consuming fire has been domesticated into a candle flame, adding a bit of religious atmosphere, perhaps, but no heat, no blinding light, no power for purification.

When the true story gets told, whether in the partial light of historical perspective or in the perfect light of eternity, it may well be revealed that the worst sin of the church at the end of the twentieth century has been the trivialization of God.

"Why do people in churches seem like cheerful, brainless tourists on a packaged tour of the Absolute?" asks Annie Dillard.

On the whole, I do not find Christians, outside the catacombs, sufficiently sensible of the conditions. Does anyone have the foggiest idea what sort of power we so blithely invoke? Or, as I suspect, does no one believe a word of it? The churches are children playing on the floor with their chemistry sets, mixing up a batch of TNT to kill a Sunday morning. It is madness to wear ladies' straw hats and velvet hats to church; we should all be wearing crash helmets. Ushers should issue life preservers and signal flares; they should lash us to our pews. For the sleeping god may wake some day and take offense, or the waking god may draw us out to where we can never return.[1]

We prefer the illusion of a safer deity, and so we have pared God down to more manageable proportions. Our era has no exclusive claim to the trivialization of God. This has always been *the* temptation and *the* failure for the people of God. Pagan gods have caused less trouble than the tendency to re-fashion God into a more congenial, serviceable god.

FROM GOD TO GOLDEN CALF

Somewhere around 1350 to 1200 BC, God liberated a ragtag group of Hebrew slaves from Egyptian bondage and then revealed through Moses how saved people ought to live. As an introduction to these instructions, which we now call the Ten Commandments, God reminded them of something important: "I am the LORD your God, who brought you out of the land of Egypt, out of the house of slavery." It's as though God was saying, "Don't forget I am the God of salvation; no other god can save, no other god can deliver from bondage. You must stay centered in me to live."

Therefore . . . "You shall have no other gods before me." This commandment was given first for a reason: it is foundational for all that follows. And the second expands on the first: "You shall not make for yourself an idol, whether in the form of anything that is in heaven above, or that is on the earth beneath, or that is in the water under the earth." Those who turn from God have nothing but gods of their own making, and these false gods inevitably take concrete form in human life. Idolatry externalizes a false image of the divine.

Even as Moses was on the mountain receiving these commandments, the people turned from God. They lost patience. Where was the One who had led them into such a godforsaken wilderness? They wanted a god who would stay put, a god who would be useful as they journeyed toward whatever the future held.

So they imagined a different deity, and making their imagination concrete, they fashioned a golden calf. They did not think they had abandoned the God who had saved them ("These are your gods, O Israel," Aaron said, "who brought you up out of the land of Egypt"). But they re-fashioned God to fit their expectations and to service their desires. They reduced God to a more manageable deity; they exchanged the saving God for a trivial god.

It is worth noting that God gave the commandment against other gods not to pagans but to Israel, the very people of God. Being saved never guarantees worship of the true God. God can seem too distant, too slow in appearing, too unaccommodating to individual desires. The consequent longings easily seduce into adulterous liaisons with more immediately satisfying gods. But when the afternoon's diversion has passed, unfulfillment comes raging back with even greater intensity. By then, though, the marriage has been defiled, the God of salvation has been betrayed.

The history of Saved Ones—from ancient Israel to the modern church—shows a continual capitulation to the temptation to forsake God for other gods. But we may be more vulnerable than our forebears because of certain characteristics of our age.

LOSS OF AWE

When English physicist Sir Isaac Newton (1642–1727) published his theories of gravitation and motion, the universe was no longer seen as a place of God's constant intervention, but as operating according to rational, empirically discernible laws. Newton, a religious man, believed he was discovering laws established by the Creator. As the eighteenth century progressed, however, God was pushed farther into the corner. The "God of the gaps" seemed necessary only to account for certain irregularities. Before long, God was put out of work altogether by the growing confidence that all things would eventually be explained through refinements in scientific theory. All that remained was a deity who had created the clock of the universe, wound it up, and sat back to let it run its course.

Theoretical physicists in our century have broken open Newton's predictable universe with theories of relativity and quantum mechanics. "The most beautiful thing we can experience is the mysterious," Albert Einstein declared. "It is the source of all true art and science."[2] But the effects of the last two hundred years are not easily undone. Einstein also said, "Perfection of means and confusion of ends seem to characterize our age."[3] The scientific method has perfected the means for exploring the mysterious, but the means have triumphed over the ends. Confidence in the explanatory power of science has turned what mysteries remain into temporary way-stations of ignorance on the road toward a complete knowledge of all things.

Paleontologist Stephen Jay Gould summarized human life by saying, "We are because one odd group of fishes had a peculiar fin anatomy that could transform into legs for terrestrial creatures; because the earth never froze entirely during an ice age; because a small and tenuous species, arising in Africa a quarter of a million years ago, has managed, so far, to survive by hook and by crook. We may yearn for a 'higher' answer— but none exists."[4]

I am tempted to ask how Gould's scientific method has proven there is no "higher" answer; he demonstrates much religious faith, it seems to me, though not in a personal deity but in the process of empirical investigation. But that is a subject for another book. My point is simply that the scientific revolution has tended to push the mysterious—and with it God—to the edges of life. Nothing inherent in science demands this; Newton, as I said, believed he was discovering the laws of the Creator, and many devout students of creation continue in that conviction. But the consequence, intended or not, has been a crowding out of the mysterious in favor of the factual, a flattening of transcendence into the measurable data of immanence, a forced retirement of God to a benign but wholly unnecessary corner of the universe.

Natural science's challenge to transcendence has been intensified by social science. Psychology, particularly under the influence of Sigmund Freud, has convinced many that God, far from being "up there," is really a projection of the human psyche based in need and desire. And sociology, with its assumption that knowledge emerges through the dynamics of social interaction, has seemed to reduce God merely to a human construct.[5]

In place of God, we now have *control* and *explanation*. Scientific investigation requires control of relevant variables (often in laboratory settings) in order to test the reliability of theories. When results can be repeated with predictable regularity, theories graduate into laws. And explanation, in turn, supplies the knowledge for further control, and on it goes, as our mastery increases and God seems less and less necessary.

Our ancestors lived in a world of mystery—a world of uncontrollable and unexplainable forces. In Frederick Buechner's novel *Son of Laughter*, the biblical character Jacob asks,

> Who knows what makes leaves stir when there is no air
> to stir them, makes the calf seek the udder before it
> knows there are udders? . . . Who can say what causes
> women to bleed and the members of men to rise unbid-
> den or, full of shame and sadness, to fall unbidden?
> Who knows about dreams? . . . Who knows about the
> Fear [his name for God]?[6]

No one would ask these questions today. We know the answers, or at least someone does. Ignorance may exist, but only because scientists have not yet brought every part of nature under control. Given more time and money, answers will be forthcoming. If we do not yet understand AIDS, say, it must be because we have not funded enough research on the problem (a nation that can put a man on the moon can do any-thing it sets its mind to!). Get control, we believe, and expla-nations will emerge.

Because we do not easily escape the thought-patterns of our culture, this ethos of control and explanation may very well influence our view of God, tempting us to choose for ourselves a controllable god, a god who will not threaten our growing sense of mastery over the world. Such a god inspires no awe, of course, but neither does it threaten our security.

Unaccustomed as we are to mystery, we expect nothing even similar to Abram's falling on his face, Moses' hiding in terror, Isaiah's crying out, "Woe is me!" or Saul's being knocked flat. We are more like those described in a novel by Charles Williams who prefer "their religion taken mild—a pious hope, a devout ejaculation, a general sympathetic sense of a kindly universe—but nothing upsetting or bewildering, no agony, no darkness, no uncreated light."[7]

IMPATIENCE WITH SILENCE

Another reason we may be inclined to create a more service-able god for ourselves is because God has seemed pretty silent for much of our beleaguered century. Just as the Israelites decided a present idol was better than a distant God, we may prefer a god who stays with us, a god we can count on to be there for us, a god who provides some answers to our ques-tions.

Where has God been, we might wonder, during two World Wars, an unimaginable holocaust of attempted genocide, the Soviet Gulag, wars in Korea and Indochina and Central Amer-ica, conflicts in South Africa, Northern Ireland, and the Balkans? Humans may be no worse than they have ever been, but we now have the technology (thanks to our scientific "advancements") to spread death with demonic effectiveness.

Elie Wiesel, a survivor of Auschwitz and Buchenwald, tells of a Rabbi he knew in one of the camps. He was from Poland,

> a bent old man, whose lips were always trembling. He used to pray all the time, in the block, in the yard, in the

ranks. He would recite whole passages of the Talmud from memory, argue with himself, ask questions and answer himself. And one day he said to me: "It's the end. God is no longer with us."

And, as though he had repented of having spoken such words, so clipped, so cold, he added in his faint voice:

"I know. One has no right to say things like that. I know. Man is too small, too humble and inconsiderable to seek to understand the mysterious ways of God. But what can I do? I'm not a sage, one of the elect, nor a saint. I'm just an ordinary creature of flesh and blood. I've got eyes, too, and I can see what they are doing here. Where is the divine Mercy? Where is God? How can I believe, how could anyone believe, in this Merciful God?"[8]

It doesn't take a Nazi concentration camp to provoke questions like these. The relative affluence of modern life offers enough release from concerns for survival to hear a voice from the depths ask about other concerns: What does life *mean?* Why do I feel unfulfilled? How can I face death? We might also hear some answers—if we weren't so busy securing our affluence! The consequent stress is difficult, like crawling toward the bow of a boat in a storm. A wave of serious suffering may break over us—a child dies, a spouse files for divorce, a medical test reveals cancer—and while we're hanging on for dear life, with hands too wet and tired to hold on much longer, we cry out for help.

Too often we hear no reassuring voice, feel no strong arm lift us. Where is God when we are in such desperate need? The result can be a feeling of loneliness so acute, so excruciating, that we would rather not even think of God than deal with the implications of God's apparent silence.

Marilyn Monroe has become a kind of icon—a symbol, in a way—of the sensuality and emptiness of our time. Arthur Miller, in his autobiography *Timebends*, tells of his marriage to her. During the filming of *The Misfits* he watched Marilyn descend into the depths of depression and despair. He feared for her life, as he watched their growing estrangement, her paranoia, and her growing dependence on barbiturates. One evening, after a doctor had been persuaded to give her yet another shot, Miller stood watching her as she slept. "I found myself straining to imagine miracles," he reflected. "What if she were to wake and I were able to say, 'God loves you, darling,' and she were able to believe it! How I wish I still had my religion and she hers."[9]

But Miller had no religion, no God to love and protect his beloved in her growing lostness. Russell Baker, the newspaper columnist, expressed the same disillusionment. During boyhood he lost his father to an early death. "After this," he wrote, "I never cried again with any real conviction, nor expected much of anyone's God except indifference."[10]

Indifference. For some, perhaps especially for those who have suffered deeply, this word best describes God's relationship with humanity. The face of God, so eagerly sought and celebrated by the saints, seems nothing but a blank wall of deliberate disregard. Philosophers have described this as the "silence of God" (Sartre) and the "absence of God" (Jaspers); theologians have spoken of the "eclipse of God" (Buber) and even of the "death of God" (Hamilton).[11]

As God's silence has seemed to deepen through this century, other voices have multiplied and become louder. Technological innovations in communications have created an information explosion that will prove more revolutionary than the atomic explosion. The printing press started it all and the telegraph certainly increased the speed of communication, but neither Gutenberg nor Morse could have imagined the advances of recent decades: telephone, radio, television, satellite, computer, fax machine—instruments that have created a cataract of information washing over us. The average American, for example, is exposed to fifteen hundred commercial messages every day.[12] And what is now a river will rapidly grow to a flood of biblical proportions. It has been estimated that we now have only three percent of the information that will be available in 2010!

What have we gained by this development? We have facts, but do we have truth? We have megabytes, sound bites, and info bits—but do we have wisdom? "The tie between information and human purpose has been severed," declares Neil Postman, professor of communication arts and sciences at New York University. "Information appears indiscriminately, directed at no one in particular, in enormous volume and at high speeds, and disconnected from theory, meaning, or purpose."[13]

As information expands, so also does our need for an overarching Truth with the power to filter, integrate, and prioritize. More than ever, we need a Word to set all other words in a grammar of meaning.

So, our situation: a cacophony of voices, a desperate need to hear an authoritative Voice, and a God who seems too silent. No wonder we may be tempted to find a god more manifestly present, a god apparently more ready to provide guidance in a confusing world.

RAMPANT INDIVIDUALISM

A third characteristic of our modern age that makes us prone to forsake God for other gods is individualism. "Do your own thing" may be a recent cliché, but it springs from a sentiment buried deep in the American heart. Freedom is our most precious national asset, and we have defined it in personal, even individualistic, ways. Our mythical heroes are the pioneer who, with solitary resolve and resourcefulness, sets off to blaze new trails into the unknown, and the cowboy who, with nothing but his trusty horse and six shooter, rides into town, straightens things up, and with only a wave to the school marm rides out of town by himself.

This cultural mythology has influenced our religious life. Sociologist Robert Bellah and his colleagues, in their widely noted *Habits of the Heart—Individualism and Commitment in American Life,* point out that religious individualism runs very deep in the United States:

> Even in seventeenth-century Massachusetts, a personal experience of salvation was a prerequisite for acceptance as a church member. . . . But through the peculiarly

American phenomenon of revivalism, the emphasis on personal experience would eventually override all efforts at church discipline. Already in the eighteenth century, it was possible for individuals to find the form of religion that best suited their inclinations. By the nineteenth century, religious bodies had to compete in a consumers' market and grew or declined in terms of changing patterns of individual religious taste. But religious individualism in the United States could not be contained within the churches, however diverse they were. We have noted the presence of individuals who found their own way in religion even in the eighteenth century. Thomas Jefferson said, "I am a sect myself,"and Thomas Paine, "My mind is my church."[14]

In recent times, however, "what had been a pattern confined to the cultural elite has spread to significant sections of the educated middle class."[15] Bellah tells of Sheila Larson, a young nurse who describes her faith as "Sheilaism." She says, "I believe in God. I'm not a religious fanatic. I can't remember the last time I went to church. My faith has carried me a long way. It's Sheilaism. Just my own little voice."[16]

The literary critic Harold Bloom has argued that this widespread individualism means that the American Religion, regardless of its official label (e.g., Southern Baptist, Mormon, Christian Science, etc.) is really gnosticism:

Freedom, in the context of the American Religion, means being alone with God or with Jesus, the American God or the American Christ. In social reality, this translates as solitude, at least in the inmost sense. The soul stands apart, and something deeper than the soul, the Real Me or self or spark, thus is made free to be utterly alone with a God who is also quite separate and solitary, that is, a free God or God of freedom. What makes it possible for the self and God to commune so freely is that the self already is of God. . . . Whatever the social or political consequences of this vision, its imaginative strength is extraordinary. No American pragmatically feels free if she is not alone.[17]

The social and political consequences of this vision are great, judging from the increasing fragmentation of our cultural values. And the personal consequences certainly have a dark side; whatever the joy of freedom, the cost in loneliness and alienation can be very high. But my concern, once again, is with the influence this has on our image of God.

From Genesis, where we learn of God choosing the family of Abram to begin the work of redemption, through to Revelation, where we glimpse a vision of the Heavenly City in which every tear shall be wiped away, the Scriptures witness to God's work of grace taking place through and toward community. But the American church often witnesses more clearly to the individualism in our culture. Consider the cafeteria-style spirituality so common today: Christians graze from church to church, sampling various dishes, enjoying the preaching at First Presbyterian and the evening praise at Calvary Chapel and the music at All Saints Episcopal. A diet like this provides a good many vitamins, to be sure, but lacks one essential for growth—community.

Or consider the well-meant evangelical exhortation to "invite Jesus into your heart." I assume this imagery comes from Revelation 3:20 ("I am standing at the door, knocking; if you hear my voice and open the door, I will come in to you and eat with you, and you with me"). But why, on the basis of one verse, has an entire theology and language of "personal acceptance" of Jesus swamped the far more pervasive apostolic call to confess "Jesus is Lord"? The reason, I submit, is that it fits more comfortably with our American sensibilities. So long as *I* invite Jesus into *my* heart, I'm still in control of things and my personal freedom is in no way threatened.

What does this have to do with our image of God? *An individualistic Christianity leads inevitably to an individualistic god.* Those who have been suckled at the breast of American culture will not easily be weaned from the milk of individualism. A God who in any way threatens to lead us beyond our personal autonomy will likely be reduced to a more manageable size.

MORE THAN WE DESIRE, JUST WHAT WE NEED

This, then, is why we may be more vulnerable than our fore-bears to the temptation to forsake God for other gods: we have lost a sense of awe before transcendence; God has seemed especially silent at a time when other information has exploded in unimaginable ways; and as Americans, we have had bred in our bones a thorough-going individualism. We will be tempted, therefore, to create for ourselves gods who will not threaten us with transcendence, gods who will be manifestly useful in a world of confusing voices, and gods who will conform to the contours of our individualistic desires.

But what if we need more than we desire? According to the Bible, this precisely describes our situation. Our real problem, we are told, is sin—not sins, in the sense of this or that specific disobedience, but sin, a fundamental mis-orientation of our lives.

Our primordial parents first sinned, according to the biblical account of origins, when the serpent persuaded them to eat the one fruit which the Creator had forbidden them to eat. Not to worry, said the tempter, for you will not die when you eat it. "God knows that when you eat of it your eyes will be opened, and you will be like God, knowing good and evil." *You will be like God*. Sin, in its most rudimentary form, is the attempt to be like God, the attempt to seize God's place at the center and to take control. So, however sin might manifest itself in thoughts and words and actions, it is *essentially* self-centeredness.

Because self-centeredness leads inevitably away from the God of life and therefore toward death, because it leads toward the destruction not only of individuals but of creation, we need much more than our self-enclosed desires can imagine, let alone achieve. Salvation can only come from outside ourselves, from a God who transcends us, from a God who speaks a Word more authoritative than all human words, from a God who delivers us from the individualism that will be the death of us.

In the following chapters, we will see that the God and Father of Jesus Christ, the God whom we meet in the witness of Scripture, is more than adequate for our needs. This God is holy: that is, wholly other than us—a God, therefore, before

whom we may and must be in awe. This God, moreover, is
fully revealed through Jesus Christ—a God, therefore, who
has spoken the one necessary Word we must hear and obey.
And through Jesus Christ, the holiness of God is revealed to
be an aggressive, pursuing love—a God, therefore, who will
not leave us in lonely isolation but through the Holy Spirit
will draw us into a gracious community of divine and human
fellowship.

A God such as this will never be manageable—and may
at first be frightening. But the Bible tells us, "the fear of the
LORD is the beginning of wisdom" (Proverbs 9:10). Not craven
fear, but awe-filled fear. In his fantasy *The Wind in the Willows*,
Kenneth Grahame captures the sort of fear appropriate in the
presence of holiness:

> "This is the place of my song-dream, the place the
> music played to me," whispered the Rat, as if in a
> trance. "Here, in this holy place, here if anywhere,
> surely we shall find Him!"
>
> Then suddenly the Mole felt a great Awe fall upon
> him, an awe that turned his muscles to water, bowed his
> head, and rooted his feet to the ground. It was no panic
> terror—indeed he felt wonderfully at peace and
> happy—but it was an awe that smote and held him
> and, without seeing, he knew it could only mean that
> some august Presence was very, very near. . . .
>
> Perhaps he would never have dared to raise his
> eyes, but that . . . the call and the summons seemed still
> dominant and imperious. He might not refuse, were
> Death himself waiting to strike him instantly, once he
> had looked with mortal eye on things rightly kept hid-
> den. Trembling he obeyed, and raised his humble head;
> and then . . . he looked in the very eyes of the Friend
> and Helper. . . .
>
> "Rat!" he found breath to whisper, shaking. "Are
> you afraid?"
>
> "Afraid?" murmured the Rat, his eyes shining with
> unutterable love. "Afraid! of Him? O, never, never! And
> yet—and yet—O, Mole, I am afraid!"

Then the two animals, crouching to the earth,
bowed their heads and did worship.[18]

Trivial gods will never turn muscles to water, bow heads, and root feet to the ground. But neither will they fill us with wonder-full awe in the presence of the only Friend and Helper who can save us.

CHAPTER TWO

A Pantheon of Deities

braham Lincoln was once asked if he thought God was on the side of the North in the Civil War. He responded, "The real question is not whether God is on our side, but whether we are on God's side." More than a century later, that question remains critical.

In this chapter and the next, we will topple some trivial gods we have co-opted in response to the loss of awe, impatience with God, and individualism of our day. Three of the most popular deities in this pantheon are god-of-my-cause, god-of-my-understanding, and god-of-my-experience.

GOD OF MY CAUSE

Limping toward the end of the twentieth century, the problems that stagger our gait are many and large: ethnic and religious conflict, destruction of the environment, proliferation of demonically effective weapons, oppression of corrupt political and economic systems, fragmentation of families, devastation of inner cities—to name just a few. It ought to be difficult for any thinking person to sleep at night.

When faced with a tough challenge, it's natural to want help. I think of it as the *David Syndrome*. In the days when my only concerns were about batting averages and baseball cards, my buddies and I spent a good deal of time at Adams Playfield. As teams were chosen, an argument would usually break out. It was always about David, who could hit farther, pitch harder, and field better than any kid in the neighborhood. We always wanted him on our side; he pretty much assured victory. The challenges may now be greater and the stakes higher, but I haven't grown out of wanting a David on my side. I doubt I'm alone in this desire.

The bigger the problem, of course, the bigger the help needed, and God is the Biggest Help available. So God naturally gets called in to lend almighty support to various causes. This seems entirely proper, given the Bible's witness to God as One who holds the earth with concern, One who calls us to loose the bonds of injustice, let the oppressed go free, share our bread with the hungry, and bring the homeless poor into our houses.[1] What could be more appropriate than seeking God's help with these things?

Indeed, this must please the God revealed in Scripture—so long as a subtle shift does not take place. What can happen is this: instead of serving God by working for a just cause, we serve a just cause by using God. The cause pushes God aside; the divine end becomes simply a useful means, and God gets trivialized. With the best of motives, we throw golden rings and bracelets of passionate concern into the fire, and a calf appears to lead the way to the Promised Land of social righteousness.

The movement known as liberation theology has developed, in the last twenty years, into a more nuanced pattern of thought than its caricatures indicate. Without doubt, it has shed light on important streams in the biblical witness. But in its extremes it has often seemed more interested in the cause of liberating the oppressed than in trying to understand the God who liberates. It has tended to become captive to political and economic assumptions that have taken precedence over Scripture itself.

So Gustavo Gutierrez, one of the earliest and most influential liberation theologians, in his *A Theology of Liberation*, reads the Exodus story as a paradigm for the struggle against oppression: "The liberation of Israel is a political action. . . . Sent by Yahweh, Moses began a long, hard struggle for the liberation of his people. . . . A gradual pedagogy of success and failures would be necessary for the Jewish people to become aware of the roots of their oppression, to struggle against it."[2] The most sympathetic exegete to the cause of liberation may well question whether this is the point of the Exodus story. Is it really about the oppressed struggling against their oppressors? Or is it about a dramatic intervention of a liberating God who decided to save Israel? Lesslie Newbigin has pointed out that in much liberation theology Scripture functions only within the framework of a Marxist interpretation of history, and that the real kernel of Scripture is seen to be whatever serves the cause of the oppressed. The irony is that "if the appeal is not to revelation as found in Scripture, but to the knowledge of human affairs which is available to observation and reason, a good case could be made for asserting that the poor are simply those who have failed in the struggle for existence and—in the interests of the race—will be eliminated by those who demonstrate their fitness to survive."[3]

More is at stake here than hermeneutics. If God is brought in secondarily, after the problem (oppression) and solution (political and economic liberation) have been defined, that will invariably shape our image of God. We may view God, for example, as simply an aid to fulfilling our human aspirations, simply Big Help for what is essentially a human struggle for self-improvement.

In a similar way, feminist theology begins with the cause of counteracting the perceived damage of patriarchy. Traditional theology has failed, feminists contend, not simply because it implies God is male but because it seems to justify a hierarchical view of the world conceived in terms of powerful/powerless, superior/inferior, active/passive, and male/female.[4] The only acceptable image of God, therefore, will be one that helps eradicate the evils of patriarchy. A sovereign God who is Lord must be ruled out in favor of a God more helpful to the cause. Rosemary Radford Ruether, perhaps the leading feminist writer today, defines her God/ess as the Primal Matrix, "the great womb within which all things, gods and humans, sky and earth, human and nonhuman beings are generated."[5]

I do not wish to dispute whatever helpful truths liberation and feminist theologies have to teach. My concern is more fundamental: both begin with a cause (in some cases a good and worthy cause) and then re-conceive God accordingly. The theological enterprise flows not from divine revelation but from human evaluation; it begins not with God but with an analysis of what's most needed. Sallie McFague, in her book which won the 1988 American Academy of Religion Award for Excellence, *Models of God—Theology for an Ecological, Nuclear Age*, is honest and bold enough to admit she thinks "theology is *mostly* fiction: it is the elaboration of key metaphors and models" that prove most helpful in addressing particular problems. What we need today is a "holistic view of reality," and thus she proposes new models of God as Mother, Lover, and Friend.[6] Who God really *is*, in other words, shouldn't concern us; what matters is finding an image of God that will be useful.

Now, this approach might be fine—*if* we could be sure our analysis of the human situation was perfectly accurate. In that case, I suppose, we might assume a certain correspondence between human need and divine aid, we might reasonably argue "from below," working our way from earth to heaven. But how often do we perceive the *real* issues and needs of our time? History makes a compelling case for human blindness and self-deception. Reinhold Niebuhr wrote, "Nothing which is true or beautiful or good makes complete sense in any immediate context of history; therefore we must be saved by faith"[7]—faith, I would add, in a God who transcends history, who knows the beginning from end, who holds the truth of any problem in the context of all truth.

Seeking salvation from any other god will come to grief, for a god pressed into the service of a particular cause will be a god too trivial to offer significant help.

GOD OF MY UNDERSTANDING

A child at the beach digs a hole in the sand and, with her little bucket, busily sets about transferring the ocean into it. We smile at the grandeur of her ambition, but only because we know she will soon mature beyond such pathetic futility. An ocean cannot be contained in any hole of any size on any continent.

And neither can God be fully contained within any theological system. Yet well-meaning Christians, in seeking to bear accurate witness to God, often become so attached to their formulations they forget the discontinuity between God and what can be said about God, they forget that only in Jesus Christ has there ever been an *exact* correspondence between God and humanity. Doctrinal lines are routinely drawn in the dirt, enemies named and challenged, and offending notions bombed in *jihads* of theological self-assuredness.

Edward John Carnell, in his inaugural address as president of the young Fuller Theological Seminary on May 17, 1955, chose as his theme, "The Glory of a Theological Seminary." According to George Marsden, he said the seminary should stand for both the truth of Christ and the spirit of Christ, and he concluded by emphasizing that the crowning glory of the seminary must be its spirit of tolerance.

> Students must be taught "an attitude of tolerance and forgiveness toward individuals whose doctrinal convictions are at variance with those that inhere in the institution itself". . . . The "logic of intolerance," he said, "is deceptively simple." It is founded on spiritual and intellectual arrogance. It forgets that truth is a gift from God and that, while we must make all sorts of *provisional* judgments to maintain the home, the church, or society, final judgments of the heart are reserved for God. The clinching argument was to consider the command to "love your neighbor as yourself" and then to look at the condition of your own heart. Even Jesus' disciples cried "Is it I?" in recognition of their inability to know the inner mysteries of their own hearts. How much less are we able to pass final judgment on the mysteries of the heart of another. We do indeed have "final truth," as the fundamentalists were prone to say. But one such unquestionable truth was "Love your neighbor as yourself."

This divine command was "both a final truth and a final reason why we should be tolerant of others."[8]

The young president had barely put away his academic regalia before being accosted by an angry segment of the faculty. They had never known him to speak or write an unorthodox word, but talk about love and the limits of knowledge raised a red flag warning that heresy could not be far behind. Not only was his speech withheld from publication, Marsden notes, but "Carnell's presidency never recovered from the blow."[9]

Fuller Theological Seminary has happily moved beyond such narrowness, but this bit of history illustrates how something as basic to the Gospel-truth as love for others can be trampled by fear of theological incorrectness. An honest desire to think and speak accurately about God moves, too easily it seems, to a presumptuous conviction that our affirmations contain the whole truth about God, which has the practical effect of confining God to our truth statements. No one, of course, would say that his or her confessional statements in any way limit God; formal acknowledgment of the transcendence of God, after all, is an important part of the foundation of most theological structures. But the *practical effect*—the unintended consequence!—is to imprison God within the structure we have built, for confidence in its design and adequacy leads to the assumption that God would feel very much at home in it. And then it's a very short step to believing that God would not feel at home anywhere else.

Those who differ, therefore, must be opposed. How can you have fellowship with someone standing outside the proper theological structure, and thus outside God? The vehemence of the debate over controversial issues—such as language about God, the inerrancy of Scripture, abortion, creation and evolution, the role of women in leadership, ordination of homosexuals, and others—too often breeds arrogant certainty. Instead of an enriching exchange leading to greater discernment, we have shouting matches that shut off dialogue and fragment the Christian community. One must ask: Who is being served in all this—God or the god-of-my-understanding?

Theological confession and debate certainly have an important place in the life of the church. But all affirmations about God must be held in humility and gentleness. "Mystery withers at the very touch of force," Diogenes Allen has reminded us.

> This is a law, a truth that governs us as firmly as any law we have met so far, and as firmly as any that exists in all the permutations of matter and energy. When we treat other people as objects subordinate to our goals, their mystery has no effect on us. The larger mystery into which genuine personal encounter can lead us never becomes open to us.[10]

And what is true in human relationships is also true of the divine-human relationship. The mystery of God, in itself, cannot wither through anything we do, but surely it can wither *for us* through our forceful and confident declarations about God. Once the last plank of our theological house has been firmly nailed down, we may discover that the only god we have contained is too trivial to be worth the effort, that God "does not dwell in houses made with human hands; as the prophet says, 'Heaven is my throne, and the earth is my footstool. What kind of house will you build for me, says the Lord, or what is the place of my rest?'" (Acts 7:48-49).

The theological enterprise demands humility as much as critical thinking. The best theologians have known this. Thomas Aquinas, after completing thirty-eight treatises, three thousand articles, and ten thousand objections of his *Summa Theologica*—one of the greatest intellectual achievements of western civilization—abruptly quit his work on December 6, 1273. He had had a profound experience while celebrating Mass in the chapel of Saint Nicholas, and he announced to his secretary that he would write no more. "I can do no more," he tried to explain, "such things have been revealed to me that all I have written seems to me as so much straw."[11]

And in our own century, Karl Barth, whose writings were almost twice as long as Thomas' *Summa*, imagined entering heaven with a pushcart full of his books and hearing the angels laugh at him. "In heaven," he said, "we shall know all that is necessary, and we shall not have to write on paper or read any more. . . . Indeed, I shall be able to dump even the *Church Dogmatics*, over the growth of which the angels have long been amazed, on some heavenly floor as a pile of waste paper."[12]

Our theological systems may succeed in containing the god-of-my-understanding, but never the holy God.

GOD OF MY EXPERIENCE

Another deity with enormous power to turn us from God is the god-of-my-experience. The things we experience, naturally, are the things of which we are most certain. So *my* form of worship and *my* style of prayer and *my* focus in service easily shape the pattern into which I squeeze spiritual reality. The subjective, in other words, never has trouble overwhelming the objective.

As a boy I attended a Bible camp run by a Pentecostal denomination. Along with the swimming and late night high-jinks and homesickness were the morning and evening chapel services we were required to attend. The preaching—filled with interesting stories, as I recall—aimed for our conversion and baptism in the Holy Spirit. To show our desire for both, we were urged to "go forward" during the altar call. Most of us did, again and again. I knew I was already a Christian, but since I had not yet spoken in tongues and therefore had not been baptized in the Holy Spirit, I felt I was only about half-a-Christian.

One night I knelt for what seemed like enough time for God to turn me into a certified saint let alone make me speak in tongues. A counselor did his best to help me: he prayed over me, laid hands on me, suggested syllables for me to mouth, and held up my arms when they got weary. But he himself got tired, I suppose, and at one point in the ordeal I heard him whisper to someone who walked by, "He really doesn't want it." *He really doesn't want it.* Imagine what those words did to a boy trying his best to please God! How could I not want *it*? How could I not want the *Holy Spirit*?

I like to think I've grown beyond that wounding of my soul, but I don't need a psychologist to tell me it has left a raw nerve to this day. I felt it flare up recently when a woman sat in my office and began the conversation by saying, "Pastor, some of us were wondering whether it would be possible *really* to worship God in this church." I knew what she wanted, but I forced her to stammer it out: she wanted a particular style of worship, a more intense emotional experience with certain praise choruses and speaking in tongues. Anything other than this, in her thinking, could not be genuine worship.

The Pentecostal tradition (including its more contemporary expressions, such as the charismatic and "third wave" movements) has rendered valuable service in witnessing to the presence and power of the Holy Spirit and in showing that authentic faith touches the whole person, including the emotions. But in stressing this side of Christianity, it has tended to elevate certain experiences as the standard for authentic spirituality. Speaking in tongues, for example, has often been promoted from its New Testament status as one of the gifts of the Spirit to *the* definitive sign of being baptized in the Spirit. Dennis and Rita Bennett, early leaders in the charismatic movement, responded to the question "Can I receive the Holy Spirit without speaking in tongues?" by saying, "It comes with the package! Speaking in tongues is not the baptism in the Holy Spirit, but it is what happens when and as you are baptized in the Spirit. . . . [If] you want the free and full outpouring that is the baptism in the Holy Spirit, you must expect it to happen. . . ."[13]

I have no doubt that some people have been given the ability to pray in ecstatic utterance as a sign of the Spirit's presence; the New Testament validates this spiritual gift (1 Corinthians 14), and I have many friends who testify to its importance in their lives. But there is scant biblical evidence for turning this into a necessary proof of the spirit-filled life—so little, in fact, that most of the church for most of its history has seen this manifestation of the Spirit as one of the least important.[14] What has happened, it seems, is that some have been so moved and helped by this gift, they have not only wanted others to share in their experience but have made it normative for everyone. Those who lack the experience must therefore lack the fullness of the Spirit, which is another way of saying they lack the presence of God.

Both the counselor-of-my-youth and the woman-of-my-congregation assumed that the presence of God would always be shown in a certain experience, and thus without that experience, God could not really be present—at least not fully. Not only does this assumption contradict the fact that the God revealed in Scripture seems to love diversity—a God who didn't stop with a thousand or so insects but conjured up 300,000 species of beetles and weevils alone, a God who spoke "in many and various ways by the prophets" (Hebrews 1:1), a God revealed in the Galilean who called individuals to himself in very distinct ways—it also has the effect of limiting God, setting boundaries on the way God works in this world.

John Killinger repeats a story he heard D. T. Niles tell at the sesquicentennial celebration of Princeton University:

> Sometime after World War II, [Niles] said, during the reconstruction of Europe, the World Council of Churches wanted to see how its money was being spent in some remote parts of the Balkan peninsula. Accordingly it dispatched John Mackie, who was then the president of the Church of Scotland, and two brothers in the cloth of another denomination—a rather severe and pietistic denomination—to take a jeep and travel to some of the villages where the funds were being disbursed.
>
> One afternoon Dr. Mackie and the other two clergymen went to call on the Orthodox priest in a small Greek village. The priest was overjoyed to see them, and was eager to pay his respects. Immediately, he produced a box of Havana cigars, a great treasure in those days, and offered each of his guests a cigar. Dr. Mackie took one, bit the end off, lit it, puffed a few puffs, and said how good it was. The other gentlemen looked horrified and said, "No, thank you, we don't smoke."
>
> Realizing he had somehow offended the two who refused, the priest was anxious to make amends. So he excused himself and reappeared in a few minutes with a flagon of his choicest wine. Dr. Mackie took a glassful, sniffed it like a connoisseur, sipped it and praised its quality. Soon he asked for another glass. His companions, however, drew themselves back even more notice-

ably than before and said, "No, thank you, we don't drink!"

Later, when the three men were in the jeep again, making their way up the rough road out of the village, the two pious clergymen turned upon Dr. Mackie with a vengeance. "Dr. Mackie," they insisted, "do you mean to tell us that you are the president of the Church of Scotland and an officer of the World Council of Churches and you smoke and drink?"

Dr. Mackie had had all he could take, and his Scottish temper got the better of him. "No, dammit, I don't," he said, "but *somebody* had to be a Christian!"[15]

How easy it is to define authentic spirituality according to my particular experience and expression of it! And when I do, I end up with a very different god from the one revealed in Christ, a god whose transcendent objectivity has been pared down to the contours of my subjectivity, a god, consequently, too trivial to lift me out of my self and beyond the distortions of my flawed experience.

GOD BEYOND MY VIEW OF GOD

The examples I have given of the god-of-my-cause, the god-of-my-understanding, and the god-of-my-experience are not intended to imply that one is a problem for liberals, another for evangelicals, and another for charismatics—though I do think liberals may be more vulnerable to the god of political correctness, evangelicals more vulnerable to the god of theological correctness, and charismatics more vulnerable to the god of experiential correctness. In truth, though, we are all susceptible to being tempted by these trivial gods.

Concerns held with passionate conviction, theologies that provide a helpful intellectual framework, and formative spiritual experiences are not bad. A healthy Christian faith will have all these things! They can be lenses through which we see important aspects of the being of God. The problem arises when we forget the vast difference between our *view* of God and the *reality* of God, when we equate the picture in the lens with the whole of divine truth.

Any god I use to support my latest cause, or who fits comfortably within my understanding or experience, will be a god no larger than I and thus not able to save me from my sin or inspire my worship or empower my service. Any god who fits the contours of *me* will never really transcend me, never really be God. Any god who doesn't kick the bars out of the prison of my perceptions will be nothing but a trivial god.

CHAPTER THREE

In the Temple of Idols

A mong the astonishing convulsions of the twentieth century are two great revolutions: one set in motion by Karl Marx, the other by Sigmund Freud. With the collapse of communism, the first has waned; with the psychologizing of contemporary life, the second has waxed stronger and stronger. Os Guinness points out, "more than five hundred brand-name therapies now jostle to compete for millions of clients in an expanding market of McFreud franchises and independent outlets that pulls in more than $4 billion a year. In America today it is more hazardous to believe you are not sick than to believe you are. The couch has become as American as the baseball diamond and the golden arches."[1]

Psychology is no longer the province of arcane theorizing by European intellectuals or the luxury of those able to afford professional consolation for troubled egos. Now we all know we're either in recovery or in denial, and fearing the latter as much as our grandparents feared hell, we're rehabilitating our psyches with the intensity of Olympic milers on the last lap. We're getting in touch with abused inner children who have caused depressions and anxieties and compulsions, not to mention neuroses and psychoses, and we're joining support groups that take us through twelve steps and role playing and primal screams toward a positive self-esteem in order to maximize our human potential.

Much good comes from this: drawing upon insights from psychology, whether with a psychotherapist or in a support group or by individual study, many have found greater well-being by taking courageous steps toward self-understanding and healing. But without denying these benefits, it's worthwhile observing the extent of psychology's influence in our culture. Eighty million Americans have sought help from therapists, and an estimated ten million do so every year. In 1968 the United States had twelve thousand clinical psychologists; today we have more than forty thousand.[2] A character in one of Peter DeVries' short stories observes that "there was a time when we were afraid of being caught doing something sinful in front of our ministers. Now we are afraid of being immature in front of our therapists."[3]

The church, more often influenced by cultural trends than theological commitments, has eagerly reclined upon the psychotherapist's couch. At first, liberals fell under the spell of the pastoral counseling movement; Carl Rogers became far more important than Karl Barth. But in recent years, evangelicals have out-distanced liberals, exchanging the language of Scripture for the language of *Psychology Today*. Now sin is low self-esteem; justification refers to experiencing God's affirmation; sanctification means accepting self-worth. Pastors and theologians were once the most revered authorities in the church; today Christian psychologists have ascended the pedestal. Peruse the catalogue of almost any Christian publisher or walk down the aisle of the Christian Booksellers Association convention and you will quickly discover what's hot and what's not: what's hot is the counsel of psychologists about anxiety and addiction, depression and dependency, self-esteem and sexuality, parenting and personality disorders; what's not is the call of Jesus to deny ourselves, take up our crosses, and follow him in the way of servanthood.

In 1966 Philip Rieff offered an important cultural critique in a book called *The Triumph of the Therapeutic*.[4] The title aptly describes what has happened not only in contemporary Western culture but also in the church. Our obsession with self has led us astray into the temple of idols: in particular, god-of-my-comfort, god-of-my-success, and god-of-my-nation.

GOD OF MY COMFORT

The tendency to psychologize life has changed our view of ministry. Although the gospel calls for self-surrender in faith and obedience—an obedience that leads to a cross—we now seek to reach the "unchurched" by meeting their "felt needs."

Princeton sociologist Robert Wuthnow, describing the impact of the small group movement in the church, comments,

> At one time theologians argued that the chief purpose of humankind was to glorify God. Now it would seem that the logic has been reversed: the chief purpose of God is to glorify humankind. Spirituality no longer is true or good because it meets absolute standards of truth or goodness, but because it helps me get along. I am the judge of its worth. If it helps me find a vacant parking space, I know my spirituality is on the right track. If it leads me into the wilderness, calling me to face dangers I would rather not deal with at all, then it is a form of spirituality I am unlikely to choose.[5]

The congregation I pastored for fourteen years has programs to comfort the sick, the grieving, and the divorcing; to assist the unemployed and the over-worked; to support singles and strengthen families; to feed the hungry, clothe the naked, and house the homeless. All this is good, I'm sure, but sometimes I wonder if we've built an elaborate house of ministry on a very shaky foundation, on the curious assumption that if we dust off and patch up an individual's self, that self will more readily be denied in order to follow Christ. Why would anyone want salvation if a little re-adjustment will do? Perhaps this is why today we rarely hear the church speaking the language of conversion (e.g., "born again," "new life in Christ"); instead, its lingua franca is rehabilitation (e.g., "renewed," "journeying toward wholeness," "discovering meaning"). Christian ministry has become an effort to help people cope with their problems well enough to find a bit of happiness.

God isn't ignored in all this, of course, but is brought in to help, rather like a Great Therapist consulted to ameliorate life's difficulties. Which brings us to the real problem: the triumph of the therapeutic in the culture has led to the triumph of the therapeutic god in the church. God has been trivialized into the god-of-my-comfort, the god who will help me get what I want. Psychologist Kim Hall said, "People walk into my office and say they are Christians, but I see no difference except that they want to be happy and now expect *God* to make it so."[6]

A god like this may be useful, at least in the short run, for it can baptize wishful thinking into something that, at its best, provides energy to get through tough times. That may count for something. But sooner or later, the limitations of this god become pretty clear: this deity is nothing other than a projection of my ego, an extrapolation of my desires.

But what if our desires are part of the problem? What if ambition or lust or greed—or simply imperfect knowledge of the good—propel our desires toward destructive goals? Even a cursory observation of human life reveals that nothing, save perhaps breathing, happens with greater frequency. The reason is sin—the radical self-centeredness at the core of our beings. This preoccupation with self has to be destroyed if we are to be saved. Any god who promises to fulfill all of our desires is the devil in disguise.

Trivializing the holy God into the god-of-my-comfort sometimes happens, it should be noted, because of misapplications of Scripture. The Bible affirms that "God is love," and we might assume that a loving God would want to deliver us from all discomfort. But the highest form of love sometimes wills the suffering of the beloved, if suffering is what the beloved needs. The Bible makes it very clear that God's love for us can bring pain as well as joy into our lives. The writer to the Hebrews counsels:

"My child, do not regard lightly the discipline of the
Lord, or lose heart when you are punished by him; for

the Lord disciplines those whom he loves, and chastises every child whom he accepts." . . . [H]e disciplines us for our good, in order that we may share his holiness. Now, discipline always seems painful rather than pleasant at the time, but later it yields the peaceful fruit of righteousness to those who have been trained by it. (12:5-6,10-11)

The god-of-my-comfort may seem loving, but it's a kind of love we can do without. Any god who promises deliverance from all suffering and fulfillment of all desires is a quack whose therapies only worsen the disease. We need a Great Physician with perfect knowledge of the good, passionate love that wills it, and adequate power to accomplish it.

GOD OF MY SUCCESS

In the pernicious family of trivial gods, the god-of-my-comfort has a near relative in the god-of-my-success. This false deity enjoys great popularity in North American culture, for, in the words of William James, the "worship of the bitch-goddess success is our national disease."

Russell Baker, in his memoirs, tells of his years as a correspondent in London:

In London, I was at the top of the ladder and enjoying excessive praise from Baltimore. All ambition seemed to have been satisfied. My mother had taught if I worked hard I could amount to something, could make something of myself. She had been proved right, yet I was vaguely dissatisfied. . . . Though I couldn't put this uneasiness in words, I felt that success ought to make life more satisfying, ought to bring a peace of mind, a maturity, a serenity toward life, which I did not feel. . . . I was discovering, though I didn't realize it then, that hunger for success was bred so deeply into so many Depression youngsters that we were powerless to stop chasing it long after we had achieved it.[8]

What Baker says of his generation could also be said of the next; "baby boomers," with their quest for BMWs, designer babies, and perfect bodies, show all the signs of relentless yearning for success. No wonder pollster Lou Harris tells us that 86 percent of Americans are chronically stressed out.[9] Which of course is good news for those seeking success in the pharmaceutical market, because Americans, to cope with their stress, consume about thirty tons of aspirins, tranquilizers, and sleeping pills every day.[10] James Thurber's comment about Harold Ross may be true of many of us: "He lived at the corner of work and worry."[11]

The drive for success is relentless, and many of us are trapped on that treadmill of self-destruction. As we run faster and faster, an inner voice whispers that we're really not getting anywhere, and that makes us run even harder. It's not easy trying to live the American Dream. As someone observed, it's tough to climb the ladder of success, especially if you're trying to keep your nose to the grindstone, your shoulder to the wheel, your eye on the ball, and your ear to the ground.

We could use some help. So to solace stress, we call on God to secure success. Around our desires we drape a prayer shawl of piety, reminding ourselves that Jesus said, "Ask, and it will be given you. . . . If you then, who are evil, know how to give good gifts to your children, how much more will your Father in heaven give good things to those who ask him!" (Matthew 7:7,11). Claiming this promise, we ask . . . and ask—and feel pretty spiritual about it.

There is nothing wrong with this asking; our Lord tells us to do it. An important difference exists, however, between a childlike dependence on God and a childish badgering of God. If desires remain forever focused on visible signs of success, if attention never lifts from the gifts we seek to the Giver we ask, we will never grow beyond an immature view of the Father. It may be appropriate for a four-year-old to see her daddy primarily as a source for candy, but one would hope a forty-year-old would have a more complete view of him.

The prayer shawl may be in place, but it covers a secret desire for a Management Consultant, Financial Advisor, and

Personal Trainer—all in one mighty being who will pull us up, up, up! Sometimes the desire is not so secret; the following book titles reflect a recent trend linking the gospel to personal affluence: Kenneth and Gloria Copeland's *The Law of Prosperity* (1974); Kenneth Hagin's *How to Write Your Own Ticket with God* (1979) and *You Can Have What You Say* (1979); Joe Magliato's *The Wall Street Gospel* (1979); Kenneth Hagin, Jr.'s *How God Taught Me About Prosperity* (1980); Elbert Willis' *God's Plan for Financial Prosperity* (1982); and Jerry Savelle's *Living in Divine Prosperity* (1987).[12]

Gloria Copeland has written confidently that "the Word of God simply reveals that lack and poverty are not in line with God's will for the obedient. . . . Allow the Holy Spirit to minister the truth to your spirit until you know beyond doubt that *God's Will is Prosperity*."[13] (She means the kind of prosperity that can be converted into hard cash—as in diamond rings, luxury cars, and big houses.) The chief business of her God is to ensure material prosperity.

Gloria Copeland's religion, it seems to me, differs little from that of the fifty Japanese engineers who held a temple ceremony in 1990 to pay homage to worn-out computer chips. A large lacquer tray overflowing with used parts waiting to be exported to heaven lay before a large cross-legged Buddha, as the chief priest bowed low and chanted the *sutra*. Shogen Kobayashi said he had "no doubt that revering the chip will pay off for the Japanese people."[14] If prosperity is your goal, it makes perfect sense to worship any god who will "pay off"— whether a computer chip or the equally trivial god-of-my-success. The latter may be described and addressed in recognizably Christian language, but in fact has little to do with the God we meet in Scripture.

Even if the god-of-my-success had the power ascribed by our longings and could deliver the goods we desire, we would still find ourselves sorely in need of a God who could save us. Success, as many have discovered, isn't the salvation it's cracked up to be. Dan Wakefield's first novel, *Going All the Way*, was published in 1970. It was chosen as a Duo Main Selection of the Literary Guild, hit the *Time* magazine bestseller list for three weeks, and sold more than 800,000 copies in paperback.

Wakefield said of his success,

> The dream of a lifetime had been realized, and I was
> delighted. I was also nervous and anxious. . . . I learned
> what people have testified since the beginning of time,
> but that no one really believes until he has the
> experience—success and achievement and rewards are
> all fine, but they do not transform you, do not bring
> about a state of built-in contentment or inner peace or
> security, much less salvation. . . . The novel was not The
> Answer to all of life's problems. I had another drink.[15]

Another writer, far more widely known than Wakefield,
had a similar experience, slipping into horrible depression fol-
lowing widespread acclaim of his work. The author was J. B.
Phillips and the book was his beloved paraphrase of the New
Testament. He later wrote an autobiography titled, *The Price of
Success*.[16]

God knows we need to be lifted far higher than the ladder
of success reaches; we need to be raised above petty desires for
money and power and social status. A trivial god can sponsor
only the most trivial forms of success. But the holy God, tran-
scending all things and unhindered by a limited perspective,
can discern and deliver authentic success. To lift us to this level,
to help us become all that we can be, calls for a radical
redefinition of "success." The God who sent the beloved Son to
reveal abundant life and let him die poor, powerless, and
despised on a Roman cross has done precisely that: by declar-
ing this death a victorious ending to a perfect life, God has not
only redefined success for all time but has sent the god-of-my-
success tumbling to the bottom of the ladder.

GOD OF MY NATION

A survey of some of the most prominent deities in the temple
of triviality would be incomplete without mentioning the god-
of-my-nation. A particular favorite in the United States, this god
has incited both good and evil. The best gift offered at its altar
is patriotic sacrifice, and the worst, xenophobic violence.

The oxygen in the bloodstream of the religion devoted to the god-of-my-nation is the myth of a Christian America. How often have we heard exhortations to get this country back to its Christian roots? From pulpits to backyard conversations, from newspaper editorials to political campaigns, the lament is the same: we have drifted from our Christian heritage and now must reclaim our God-given status as a "light to the nations."

As with any powerful myth, truth and error commingle here. The colonists who first settled along the eastern shore of North America in the seventeenth century were Puritans convinced of their divinely appointed mission. John Winthrop, in a sermon to his fellow passengers aboard the *Arbella* in 1630, prophesied to the future leaders of the Massachusetts Bay Colony: "Wee shall be as a Citty upon a Hill, the eies of all people are uppon us; soe that if wee shall deale falsely with our god in this worke wee have undertaken and soe cause him to withdrawe his present help from us, wee shall be made a story and a by-word through the world."[17] And Francis Higginson echoed this sentiment of divine destiny when he wrote, in *New-Englands Plantation*, "That which is our greatest comfort, and meanes of defence above all others is, that we have here the true Religion and holy Ordinances of Almightie God taught among us . . . thus we doubt not but God will be with us, and if God be with us, who can be against us?"[18]

But by the time of the American Revolution and the establishment of our nation (our *official* beginning), things had changed dramatically. Thomas Jefferson, the greatest of our "Founding Fathers," was more deist than Christian, basing his Declaration of Independence upon "Nature's God" as opposed to a revealed God. The latter, he seemed to think, opened the door to a dangerous situation in which the godly would, on the basis of revelation, seize political power for themselves. At best, Jefferson accepted only a mild form of "Christianity," going so far as to edit the gospels into a more acceptable version called "The Life and Morals of Jesus of Nazareth."

To hear some today, you would think the Constitutional Convention was an evangelical revival and that every citizen of the new country actively participated in church. Such was not the case. A comparative statistic may set things in per-spective: today, 62 percent of Americans are involved in a church, but in 1776, only 17 percent were involved.[19] Who would want to take America back to *these* roots?

Americans are now far more religious, and for the vast majority, Christianity holds a place of high honor. Russell Chandler reports the results of a 1990 survey asking 113,000 Americans to identify their religion: 86 percent claimed to be Christian, and just 7.5 percent said they had no religion at all.[20]

But actual behavior suggests that this phenomenon reflects only a sentimental preference rather than a deep commitment. A few years ago, *Self* magazine polled its readers to determine the most popular personal public heroes. Jesus made the list, to be sure, but he came in behind Mother Teresa, George Bush, Madonna, Norman Schwartzkopf, and Cher—tying with the Desert Storm Troops and Julia Roberts! James Patterson and Peter Kim, of the J. Walter Thompson advertising agency, wrote an interesting book titled, *The Day America Told the Truth: What People Really Believe About Everything That Really Matters*. The authors report results of a national survey of our habits and moral convictions. "There is," the authors conclude, "absolutely no moral consensus at all in the 1990s." Their research indicates only 13 percent of Americans believe all the Ten Commandments were binding.[21] The evidence simply does not support the view that we are a "Christian nation."

Add to this litany of concern a 1986 Gallup poll showing that for the first time the military establishment rather than the church was our most trusted institution,[22] and while you're at it, add the soaring rates for violent crime, infant mortality, homelessness, divorce, abortion, and incidents of racial bigotry. A Christian nation?

P. J. O'Rourke described pretty well the prevailing ethos of this country:

We're Americans. These are modern times. Nothing bad is going to happen to us. If we get fired, it's not failure; it's a midlife vocational reassessment period. If we screw up a marriage, we can get another one. There's no shame in divorce. Day Care will take the kids, and the

ex-wife can go back to [her career]. . . . If we get convicted of a crime, we'll go to tennis prison and probably
not even that. We'll just have to futz around doing community service for a while. Or maybe we can cheerfully
confess everything, join a support group and get off the
hook by listening to shrinks tell us we don't like ourselves enough . . . play our cards right, and we can get a
book contract out of it.[23]

Whatever else we might say about America, we certainly
cannot say it is a nation perfectly attuned to the will of a holy
God! It never has been.

It's remarkable, therefore, how many seem eager to enwrap
God in red, white, and blue bunting, how many seem convinced that, of all the nations of the world, this is God's most
beloved. What's good for America, many seem to believe, must
be good for God; there seems little practical difference, for
many sincere Christians, between the Kingdom of God and the
United States of America.

Do I exaggerate? Let me propose a test: remove from your
church sanctuary the Christian flag and watch whether anyone
even notices; then remove the U.S. flag and watch how quickly
your hide gets nailed to the wall. I did this (after twelve years
of working up the courage!), and *not one person* mentioned the
loss of the Christian flag. But at the next meeting of elders, we
had a pretty heated discussion about the absence of Old Glory.
"What happened to the flag?" one elder demanded to know. I
explained I had moved it to the narthex, the symbolic border,
as it were, between the world and the church, and I reminded
them that we are not the Rotary Club but part of a church that
pledges ultimate allegiance to a very different Commonwealth.
They decided they could live with it in the narthex, but had I
tried to remove it from the church grounds altogether, they
might have decided they could live without me.

Truth is, many in the American church are Americans first
and Christians second. They have never consciously prioritized
these loyalties, though, because it has never occurred to them
there may be a difference, let alone a conflict, between the two.
But when American patriotism is blended with Christian

spirituality, the former will always bully the latter. Patriotism, if it's anything more than sentimentalism, leads inevitably to politics. And politics has a concrete immediacy: it regulates lives, reaches into pocketbooks, opens doors for some and closes them for others. This practicality exerts a powerful gravitational pull from which our Christian commitments separate us only with great difficulty. The consequent distortion of perspective shapes our view of God.

To put it bluntly, for most evangelicals God is a Republican, and for most mainline liberals God is a Democrat. During the last national election, one organization sent out a brochure announcing the "Christian" position on many issues; I was surprised to discover that God was in favor of limiting congressional terms and lowering taxes. On the other side, study social pronouncements of mainline denominations in the last twenty years, and you will have difficulty finding a single position unsupported by the liberal wing of the Democratic Party. (Both evangelical and liberal Protestants would do well to learn from the blessed political inconsistency of the Roman Catholic bishops; when it comes to the "sanctity of life," for example, they have opposed both abortion and the nuclear arms build-up of the 1980s.)

Both deities, the one who rides an elephant and the one who rides a donkey, are trivial gods too limited by narrow interests to do anything but create a pseudo-religious atmosphere that, however handy for political huckstering, has no power to save a nation, let alone a single individual. The holy God of the Bible neither adds a *basso profundo* to "God Bless America" nor joins the raucous rendering of "Happy Days Are Here Again"; the holy God of the Bible has set apart only one nation—Israel—and that to be a "light to the nations," witnessing in its history to both the grace and the judgment of God; the holy God of the Bible transcends all boundaries, holding the whole world in the embrace of love.

Do not misunderstand me: I am grateful for the ways God has blessed America, and I believe we should express our citizenship by helping to order society according to the will of God as we understand it. But letting God define political commitments is one thing; letting political commitments define God is entirely something else. Unfortunately, the powerful pull of politics too often trivializes God into a god-of-my-nation unable to do much more than offer a misty-eyed sentimentalism.

BLIND TO THE GREATER REALITY

A couple of years ago, while vacationing in Seattle, I rented a sailboat on Lake Union. It was a beautiful day, and I was gloriously happy: the wind was blowing, the boat was scudding at high speed, and a gentle spray was breaking over the bow. If the Kingdom had not yet come, it felt very, very near.

Suddenly my reverie was ravaged by a float plane landing a few yards in front of me. My heart stopped, my body tensed with shock; a few seconds later, I trembled like a man who had seen death wink at him. I had heard and seen nothing of the approaching plane. The pilot had idled his engine to a whisper as he glided toward the water, and the sail had completely blocked my view. To my left I had seen water and the beautiful Seattle skyline, with Mt. Rainier in the background, but to my right, nothing but white dacron tautly reaching into the sky. The sail had completely blinded me. My distorted perspective had given me a false sense of security, a skewed apprehension of the true state of things.

When we trivialize God a similar thing happens: we fail to recognize that our view is only partial—however attractive or useful it seems—and we sail along insensible of the Greater Reality.

It's important to confess the presence of the sail, to admit our blindness. To know the holy God, we must acknowledge what we do not know; to see the light of God, we must pass through the dark night of the soul; to gain faith, we must begin with doubt. Knowledge of God is born from the womb of reverent agnosticism. To this paradox we now turn.

CHAPTER FOUR

In Praise
of Agnosticism

It is easy today to bemoan "the loss of faith" in our so-called secular culture. We should remember, though, that it was Israel that created the golden calf, and it is the church that prostrates itself before the illusory power of manageable deities. So each of us must take heed: our knowledge of God may not be as trustworthy as we think.

The holy God transcends all golden calves cast from earrings of misdirected imagination; the holy God, in fact, transcends all things. Between Creator and creature, as Kierkegaard said, there is an infinite qualitative difference. And this difference calls us to *reverent agnosticism*.

Does the word *agnosticism* set your hair on end? Let me explain. An agnostic, unlike an atheist, does not deny the existence of God. The term literally refers to one who says, "I do not know . . ." (from the Greek *a-gnostos*, "not-knowing"). It popularly indicates a lack of conviction concerning the reality of God, yet it also refers to any want of knowledge about God. A *reverent* agnostic, to take it a step further, may even be able to sing with the psalmist, "Great is the Lord, and greatly to be praised; his greatness is unsearchable"—so long as the emphasis falls on the last word. Agnosticism is simply a five-dollar word for ignorance.

The transcendence of God—the *wholly otherness* of God—means that we must begin by admitting that in the human attempt to know God, we're in the dark.

NO WAY AROUND AGNOSTICISM

What about Jesus Christ, you may ask, and the Bible, and the teaching of the church? Don't these reveal truth about God? Indeed they do, and we shall listen carefully to them in the remaining chapters of this book. But there is an important order to knowing. Whether we recognize it or not, we begin as agnostics. If we do not acknowledge this, we will be too preoccupied with trivial gods to notice the real God standing before us. Only by confessing complete ignorance will we be humble enough to receive a God who may be very different from the gods we have fashioned for ourselves. Only in darkness will we see the Light; only in silence will we hear the Word.

But doesn't Scripture teach that God has given, in addition to a specific revelation in Jesus Christ, a general revelation in creation discernible to all who choose to see it? Yes, Paul argues that "what can be known about God is plain. . . . Ever since the creation of the world his eternal power and divine nature, invisible though they are, have been understood and seen through the things he has made" (Romans 1:19-20). The glory of nature does not leave us completely ignorant concerning God; creation witnesses to a Creator.

The question is, What kind of Creator? About the only thing we can affirm when we look up at the grandeur of stars or down into the intricacies of cells is the power of God: 100 billion stars in our moderately sized galaxy located in a universe of 100 billion galaxies witnesses to creative power of unimaginable magnitude; the human brain, with 75 to 100 billion nerve cells, each having as many as 10,000 connections with other nerve cells, witnesses to creative power of purposeful detail.

Stay attentive to nature, though, and the situation becomes ambiguous: a black widow spider eats her mate after a sexual romp, an earthquake in Japan levels a city, a flood in Bangladesh kills tens of thousands and leaves millions homeless, cancer cells rampage through the body of a loved one—and you have to wonder about our world. Romanticism about nature might have inspired some fine English poets, but it doesn't entirely square with the facts. The ambiguity of nature was unpoetically but accurately expressed by Rodney Dangerfield when he said, "I put a seashell to my ear and got a busy signal." Yes, there is something—or Someone—on the other end of the line, but we don't hear much more than a busy signal.

Paul Davies, professor of mathematical physics, wrote, "Through my scientific work I have come to believe more and more strongly that the physical universe is put together with an ingenuity so astonishing that I cannot accept it merely as a brute fact. There must be, it seems to me, a deeper level of explanation." Those who have been persuaded by the apostle's argument in Romans would respond, "Yes, that's exactly right; creation witnesses to a Creator." But what Davies says next reveals the problem: "Whether one wishes to call that deeper level 'God' is a matter of taste and definition."[1] Creation may attest "a deeper level of explanation," but it doesn't get specific beyond that; it doesn't tell us about the character of God.

Enjoying a great painting in an art gallery, I can be moved by the artist's skill and perception and insight, but I remain ignorant of the artist himself. (Is he tall or short? Humble or arrogant?) His work tells little of his character. The firmament indeed proclaims God's handiwork, as the psalmist says, but offers scant instruction on the God whose hands did the work. The firmament, in other words, leaves us agnostic.

Actually, contemplating the firmament may increase agnosticism. The power of the Creator, so evident even without telescope or microscope, can fill us with such awe, such mind-numbing incomprehension, that we ask, "Who is this God, anyway?" Reflecting on the vastness of the universe only intensifies the mystery; there is nothing like a clear night to put us in our place and remind us that the Creator is *very* different from anything within creation; the twinkling stars contrast not only with the dark sky but with our dark minds.

To compound our difficulty, to mire us deeper in agnosticism, the perversity of human will distorts our perception of reality. Sin blinds. After speaking of creation's declaration of divine power, Paul concludes that humans are "without excuse; for though they knew God, they did not honor him as God or give thanks to him, but they became futile in their thinking and their senseless minds were darkened." The consequence of this refusal to honor God as God was the perverse exchanging of "the glory of the immortal God for images resembling a mortal human being or birds or four-footed animals or reptiles" (Romans 1:20-23). Turning our backs on God, in other words, causes night to fall on rational thought and spiritual intuition; turning away from Light, we move deeper into darkness. But we don't want to live without some sort of divine help, and so we make trivial gods to bolster sagging spirits with the lie that the darkness really isn't all that dark.

We should not infer from this that our blindness is total; sin blinds us to God but not necessarily to *all* truth. The powerful pull of self-centeredness, though skewering our overall picture of reality, does not preclude significant knowledge about creation. A physicist, for example, may be thoroughly despicable—motivated by crass ambition, say, and a hater of humanity—yet do responsible research on the density of black holes or the radiation of quasars. She cannot speak accurately about God, but that does not mean she cannot speak accurately about other things. Agnosticism about God does not entail stupidity about everything.

But sin does prevent an accurate knowledge of God's character. "God is inaccessible to both human perception and conception," writes Donald Bloesch. "God is not ontologically remote from either humanity or nature, but God is hidden in the world of empirical reality because of the blindness caused by human sin. The heavens declare and reveal the glory of God (Psalm 19:1-4), but only those with the eyes and ears of faith can see this light and hear this voice."[2]

SILENT REVERENCE

Whatever we might eventually say about God because of God's self-revelation, our thoughts and words must be formed in the profound silence of not-knowing. Our fundamental posture toward God, therefore, must be reverence. Who are we to talk about God? Who are we to imagine a being *wholly other* than our rational and intuitive capacities? At best, even after we have listened attentively to the Word God speaks and formulated as carefully as possible our theological formulations, we can do nothing but touch the hem of God's garment; our mental arms are too short to embrace Divine Mystery.[3]

You would never know this from life in most churches. Worshipers gather as though attending a football game or a movie, arriving breathless from the parking lot, laughing with ushers, waving at friends—as though it were entirely natural for humans to meet God. No big deal, it seems, to encounter the Lord of the universe. In evangelical churches the service often moves through chatty certainties about God; happy smiles radiate from smooth-talking preachers who demonstrate absolutely no reticence to speak on behalf of the Almighty. In liberal churches the language may be less certain about the being of God, but that is more than compensated by confidence about what in God's name should be done in society, so that the vertical gets flattened into the horizontal, any sense of transcendence gets banished by boring banalities; the affair has all the mystery of a meeting of the city zoning commission.

We will deal more fully with worship and proclamation later, but for now I want to stress that agnosticism should so encompass our theological affirmations that we are driven to reverent silence, to respectful concern to speak *only* about what we have been told—and then with the tone of a high school sophomore telling what she knows about vectors to a Nobel prize-winning physicist. What we say may be true enough, but so obviously spoken out of ignorance that we dare not chatter on in blissful confidence.

Many of us, though, have spent decades in a church that has inherited nearly two millennia of conversations about God, with the result that we now speak of divine matters with the ease of prattling about transmission problems in the Chevy. Perhaps it is time for a deferential hush.

Dietrich Bonhoeffer, while in prison because of his participation in the resistance against Hitler, wrote a letter to his nephew on the occasion of the infant's baptism. In it, he speculated about the future of the church in a Christendom that had had much language about God but was destroying itself through murderous warfare:

> It is not for us to prophesy the day (though it will come) when men will once more be called so to utter the word of God that the world will be changed and renewed by it. It will be a new language, perhaps quite non-religious, but liberating and redeeming—as was Jesus' language; it will shock people and yet overcome them by its power; it will be the language of a new righteousness and truth, proclaiming God's peace with men and the coming of his kingdom. . . . Till then the Christian cause will be a silent and hidden affair, but there will be those who pray and do right and wait for God's own time.[4]

To what extent the Christian cause today should become "a silent hidden affair," I'm not sure. Wading through the proliferation of Christian materials, listening to religious programming on radio and television, attempting to find a moment of reverence in a typical worship service—these things make me wonder if a temporary moratorium on religious speech wouldn't be salutary. (Even as I add another book to the vast ocean of religious print!) I *do* believe that our words about God must reflect the agnosticism of our true condition.

HUMBLE CIVILITY

Recognizing that ignorance about God is unavoidable sets us free from the burden of having to know it all. We stagger under this weight for a variety of reasons: sometimes we want an answer for every theological question in order to present a credible witness; sometimes we hope that if we understood certain things about God (e.g., why God allows evil, etc.) we would have more faith and less doubt; sometimes we simply commit intellectual hubris. But it's an impossible load to carry, and the sooner we get it off our backs the better off we'll be.

"It is a consoling idea," wrote Kierkegaard, "that before God we are always in the wrong."[5] The radical nature of sin sets us free from finding excuses and marshalling arguments to justify ourselves and worrying about the adequacy of our piety. We can relax in our guilt, as it were, and accept God's grace. Similarly, it is a consoling idea that before God we are always in the dark. We know only what we have been told, and that means we can allow ourselves to be what we truly are—what Annie Dillard calls "the faint tracing on the surface of mystery."[6]

In my early years as a pastor I would have admitted there was much about God I didn't know; in practice, though, I always *felt* I needed to have an answer when a grieving mother asked why God allowed a three-year-old to die, or an anguished student wanted to grasp the relationship between divine sovereignty and human free will, or a teenager asked for an explanation of the Trinity. Too often this meant I assumed the role of God's defense attorney, trying my best to bolster God's public approval rating. Now I'm more likely to say, "I don't know." And I feel as though I've changed from a swaybacked workhorse into a winged Pegasus; not having to carry the crushing weight of theological omniscience has been like the freedom of flight.

This freedom can have a wonderful consequence, if permitted to press its advantage in our lives: it can create a sorely needed space of civility between us and others. We live in an era when intense battles rage over the family, art, education, law, and politics. James Davison Hunter, in his widely noted *Culture Wars—The Struggle to Define America*, says these conflicts are "a struggle over national identity—*over the meaning of America*, who we have been in the past, who we are now, and perhaps most important, who we as a nation, will aspire to become in the new millennium."[7] And where is the church in all this? Torn apart, split not simply between denominations but by the much greater gulf between evangelicals and liberals.[8] Deep passions and the importance of what's at stake conspire to raise the level of discourse to a babel of arrogant certainties, as though terribly complex issues could be hammered into simplicity by increasing the volume of argument. Seldom are heard sounds of quiet humility; seldom are heard convictions expressed with the gentleness befitting those who are really agnostic in what matters most. Our culture—including the church within it—could use a massive infusion of what Richard Mouw calls "uncommon decency."[9] Confessing the agnosticism of our natural condition, admitting the ignorance at the core of whatever we think we know, could go a long way toward taming overly confident tongues.

The apostle James said, "Every species of beast and bird, of reptile and sea creature, can be tamed and has been tamed by the human species, but no one can tame the tongue—a restless evil, full of deadly poison" (James 3:7-8). I doubt rattlesnakes and mosquitoes have been tamed, but the exaggeration can be forgiven because of the indisputable truth of his main point: the tongue is often an instrument of evil, spitting its poison into relationships and rending asunder whole cultures.

I cannot promise that recognizing our ignorance of God will tame this restless little beast, but I think it can go a long way toward caging it behind bars of civility. Our attitude toward others and manner of discourse can be changed by a spirit of humility. It would be unseemly to argue about what to do with the poor of India in the presence of Mother Teresa; some circumstances demand moderation of expression if not respectful silence. When we come to know our not-knowing, when we see our blindness, when we understand the depths of our ignorance—when we freely accept our agnosticism— we may indeed find both a freedom from having to know it all and a humble civility to check our strutting tongues.

PATIENT OPENNESS

Our agnosticism, finally, obliges us to open ourselves as fully as possible to God's self-revelation. We really have no other option: we may be able to discover many things about ourselves and our world through logical reasoning and empirical science, but when it comes to God, we know only what we have been told. Faith in God, as opposed to faith in trivial gods of our own creation, demands radical receptivity, a fierce openness to hear the Word spoken to us. Preconceptions must be set aside; inner voices must be stilled. None of this comes easily or perfectly, but we must never quit trying, never quit lancing boils of easy certainties in order to receive the healing ointment of truth God applies to the open wound of our ignorance.

Freeman Patterson, an outstanding Canadian photographer, explained his method of taking pictures in a way that describes well the openness our agnosticism compels us toward:

> Letting go of the self is an essential precondition to real seeing. When you let go of yourself, you abandon any preconceptions about the subject matter which might cramp you into photographing in a certain, predetermined way. As long as you are worried about whether or not you will be able to make good pictures, or are concerned about enjoying yourself, you are unlikely either to take the best photographs you can or experience the joy of photography to the fullest. When you let go new conceptions arise from your direct experience of the subject matter, and new ideas and feelings will guide you as you make pictures.
>
> Preoccupation with self is the greatest barrier to seeing, and the hardest one to break.[10]

This sort of letting go—of preconceptions and preoccupation with self—is also necessary to have imprinted on the film of our understanding images created by *the* Light. What we know of God, we must receive from God. As Saint Augustine observed, when God gives, it is to empty hands.

CHAPTER FIVE

The Self-Revelation
of God

A t Trafalgar Square in the city of London stands a statue
of Lord Nelson. Resting atop a tall pillar, it towers too
high for passersby to distinguish his features. For this
reason, about forty years ago a new statue—an exact replica of
the original—was erected at eye level so that everyone could
see him.[1] God also transcends our ability to see; the eyes of our
understanding cannot discern divine features. But we have set
before us an exact representation, "the image of the invisible
God." To know God, we must look only at Jesus.

The bare outline of the life of Jesus, as witnessed by the
New Testament, shows what an unlikely, astonishing thing this
is. Would anyone, by summoning all powers of thought and
imagination, have dreamed of a God born not in the presence
of kings but of barnyard animals, a God mewling and messing
diapers, a God wandering around a backwater province of the
Roman Empire with an inconsequential band of followers, a
God performing mighty few miracles in the presence of much
suffering, a God rejected by pastors and theologians and the
most pious of the land, a God charged with blasphemy and
nailed to die on a cross? Who could have imagined *this* to be
the representation of God?

Clever thinking and creative imagination may conjure up pictures of divine reality, but the resulting portraits say more about us than God. They confirm Ludwig Feuerbach's assessment of religion: "God is himself the realized wish of the heart, the wish exalted to the certainty of its fulfillment . . . the secret of theology is nothing else than anthropology—the knowledge of God nothing else than the knowledge of man!"[2] Our ignorance imprisons us within ourselves, leaving us with nothing but trivial gods of our own creation.

Divine truth must come from outside us. It cannot be self-generated by us; it must be self-revealed by God. Christian faith rests on the conviction that just such a disclosure has been given in Jesus Christ. "He is the image of the invisible God. . . . [In] him the fullness of God was pleased to dwell" (Colossians 1:15,19). Methodist preacher Ralph Sockman declared that "the hinge of history" was on the door of a Bethlehem stable—because "That glorious form, that light unsufferable/ And that far-beaming gaze of majesty/ . . . Forsook the courts of everlasting day/ And chose with us a darksome house of mortal clay."[3]

KARL BARTH AND MIDDLE C

Karl Barth understood the necessity of God's self-revelation better than anyone in our time, perhaps better than anyone in the history of the church. He has been rejected by conservatives for his acceptance of biblical criticism and scorned by liberals as a biblical literalist; he has been the most influential theologian of this era, and the most consciously ignored by those fearful of his long shadow; a small library has been written about him, often by those who haven't taken the time to study him carefully. But whatever preconceived quarrels we might have with him should be set aside long enough to hear his central concern. With the passion of a prophet he trumpeted a truth we sorely need to learn: There are fundamentally only two approaches to knowing God—one that begins with humans or one that begins with God.

The first, Barth knew, was clearly expressed in the Protestant theology of the nineteenth century. This was an age of idealism, an age inspired by optimistic faith in human potential and historical progress, an age which "believed it could unite God and the world, religion and culture, faith and intellect, divine righteousness and earthly authority, throne and altar in a natural and almost unbroken harmony, and which therefore looked forward with confidence to the future."[4] Such faith in humanity led inevitably to an all-encompassing subjectivism which sought to know God by beginning with human feelings and thoughts. No theologian expressed this more transparently than Friedrich Schleiermacher: The idea of God, he wrote in *The Christian Faith*, "is nothing more than the expression of the feeling of absolute dependence."[5] He began with the sensation of being subject to a higher power; human experience, he argued, is the path toward understanding God. But this approach, Barth saw, could never lead beyond itself. To borrow an image from T. F. Torrance, subjectivism is "like a sheep over-whelmed in the snowdrift trying to keep itself alive by feeding upon its own ideas."[6]

Two things happened that proved decisive for Barth in developing this conviction. The first was World War I. A casualty of the bloody slaughter was cheerful confidence in the innate goodness of humanity. (Barth was stunned and outraged when German professors who had been influential in his intellectual development signed a manifesto in support of the Kaiser's war policies.) It had become evident that "one can *not* speak of God simply by speaking of man in a loud voice."[7] The assumption of a basic continuity between Creator and creature had to be shattered; what was needed more than anything else was to say, "God is in heaven, and thou art on earth."[8]

The second thing that happened to Barth was the pulpit. He became a pastor in Safenwil, Switzerland, and had to preach Sunday by Sunday. What would he give his people? An optimistic bromide on human potential? No, that option had been forever dashed. A report on his own intuitions about God? No, God was *totaliter aliter*—totally other—and thus inaccessible to human thought and feeling. Barth was thus driven to the conviction that he could say only what had already been said, driven to utter dependence on the Word spoken by God. In Jesus Christ he discovered news worth announcing. "In His name two worlds meet and go apart, two planes intersect, the one known and the other unknown."⁹ Therefore one can indeed speak the unspeakable and conceive the inconceivable—but *only because* of the revelation of God in Jesus Christ.

Barth's direction was set for the rest of his life. He never wavered. In lecture after lecture and book after book, he kept his attention centered on Jesus Christ, God's self-revelation born to a virgin in a Bethlehem stable and nailed to a cross outside the gates of Jerusalem. So when the shadow of Naziism spread across Europe, darkening even the church, Barth met with leaders of the Confessing Church at Barmen on May 29-31, 1934, and authored a declaration they would issue in response to the errors of the "German Christians." It was a great affirmation of evangelical truth and a fine summary of his own theological work. The first statement reads, "Jesus Christ, as he is attested for us in Holy Scripture, is the one Word of God which we have to hear and which we have to trust and obey in life and in death. We reject the false doctrine, as though the Church could and would have to acknowledge as a source of its proclamation, apart from and besides this one Word of God, still other events and powers, figures and truths, as God's revelation."¹⁰

Karl Barth powerfully witnessed to a truth we have heeded too little, a truth we have let slide as we have constructed for ourselves manageable gods to secure our desires: we know God only through Jesus Christ. No other god will ever be more than a projection of our own subjectivity, and consequently no other god will ever be more than a trivial caricature of deity.

Lloyd C. Douglas, author of *The Robe* and other novels, lived in a boarding house when he was a university student. On the first floor resided a retired music teacher, infirm and unable to leave his apartment. Every morning they had a ritual: Douglas would come down the steps, open the old man's door and ask, "Well, what's the good news?" The other would pick up his tuning fork, tap it on the side of his wheelchair, and say, "That's middle C! It was middle C yesterday; it will be middle C tomorrow; it will be middle C a thousand years from now. The tenor upstairs sings flat, the piano across the hall is out of tune, but, my friend, that is middle C!"¹¹ The old man had discovered a constant reality on which he could depend, an unchanging truth to which he could cling.

Jesus Christ is our tuning fork, ringing out middle C in a cacophonous world of competing truths; his pitch defines tonal reality and sets every other note in its proper place. Without him, truth—especially truth about God—will be distorted, disordered, disharmonious. To hear the music of heaven, therefore, we must listen to him.

When we listen to middle C two things happen: the revelation of Jesus Christ both separates us from God and unites us to God.

REVELATION SEPARATES

If knowledge of God comes to us through Jesus Christ and not through our own religious subjectivity, there can be no question about our proper place. God is in heaven, we are on earth; God speaks, we listen. We know God only in humility—the humility that ceases all attempts to storm the gates of theological truth with self-generated brain power or spirit power, the humility that refuses to go around Jesus Christ to find a more immediate revelation, the humility that simply receives what has been given to us.

John Macquarrie, in his *Principles of Christian Theology*, illustrates the danger of building a theology on a foundation of human knowing. In discussing the work of Christ, he quickly dismisses the notion of substitutionary atonement, because he sees it as "an example of the kind of doctrine which, even if it could claim support from the Bible or the history of theology, would still have to be rejected because of the affront which it offers to reason and conscience."[12] The *real* authority for John Macquarrie, it appears, is human reason, and thus it's no surprise when he says, "we see christology as a kind of transcendent anthropology."[13] This statement suggests that speaking about God can be accomplished by speaking about humanity in a loud voice.

In *The Horse and His Boy*, C. S. Lewis tells the tale of a horse, Bree, and the boy who rides him, Shasta. In their adventures they are joined by another horse, Hwin, and her young mistress,

Aravis. Toward the end of the story Bree learns something important about himself. The insight comes while he is scoffing at Aravis' suggestion that Aslan, the great deliverer of Narnia, might actually be a real lion. He fails to notice that Hwin and Aravis are staring wide-eyed at something on the wall behind him:

> [While] Bree spoke they saw an enormous lion leap up from the outside and balance itself on the top of the green wall; only it was a brighter yellow and it was bigger and more beautiful and more alarming than any lion they had ever seen. And at once it jumped down inside the wall and began approaching Bree from behind. It made no noise at all. And Hwin and Aravis couldn't make any noise themselves, no more than if they were frozen.
>
> "No doubt," continued Bree, "when they speak of him as a Lion they only mean he's as strong as a lion or (to our enemies, of course) as fierce as a lion. Or something of that kind. Even a little girl like you, Aravis, must see it would be quite absurd to suppose he is a *real* lion. Indeed it would be disrespectful. If he was a lion he'd have to be a Beast just like the rest of us. Why!" (and here Bree began to laugh) "If he was a lion he'd have four paws, and a tail, and *Whiskers!* . . . Aie, ooh, hoo-hoo! Help!"
>
> For just as he said the word *Whiskers* one of Aslan's had actually tickled his ear. Bree shot away like an arrow to the other side of the enclosure and there turned; the wall was too high for him to jump and he could fly no farther. Aravis and Hwin both started back. . . .
>
> "Now, Bree," [Aslan] said, "you poor, proud, frightened Horse, draw near. Nearer still, my son. Do not dare not to dare. Touch me. Smell me. Here are my paws, here is my tail, these are my whiskers. I am a true Beast."
>
> "Aslan," said Bree in a shaken voice, "I'm afraid I must be rather a fool."
>
> "Happy the Horse who knows that while he is still young. Or the Human either."[14]

Whenever we prattle on about what God must be like—crafting trivial gods with the pitiful tools of our thinking and imagination—we are first-class fools. But God does not leave us in blind, arrogant stupidity; the Lion of Judah jumps over our carefully constructed walls of certainty and rubs whiskers across our startled ears. He says, "Draw near. Nearer still, my sons and daughters. Do not dare not to dare. Touch me. . . ."

So God's revelation in Jesus Christ first puts us in our place, exposes our limitations, and in this sense, separates us from God. God is not as close or familiar as we had assumed. When our presumption is uncovered and the distance revealed, our initial reaction may be fright.

REVELATION UNITES

The high paradox of this exposure is that the very moment God puts us in our place becomes the moment in which God meets us in that place; the Lion who frightens says, "Touch me"; the separation becomes a profound uniting.

If the apostolic witness is true, if in Jesus Christ dwells all the fullness of God, we may be liberated from fearful anxiety that behind our rational theologizing and our pious spiritualizing exists a God dark and hidden, a God remote in inscrutability, a God before whom the knees of our soul could only shake in uncertain terror. If Jesus Christ reveals the face of God, the essential being of deity, we may with confidence seize the trustworthy knowledge of God given to us: in Jesus Christ we meet God, the God who really *is*.

Because God's self-disclosure comes through a *person*, we make the basic affirmation that *God is personal*. Whatever else we might eventually say about God, we must begin here. The God revealed in Jesus Christ acts as a "Self," an "I." "The subject of theology," in Paul Jewett's words, "is not the God who is the 'Unmoved Mover,' *'Prima Causa,'* 'Ground of Being,' 'Source of Human Ideals,' 'Vital Urge in the Evolutionary Process,' 'Ultimate Integrating Principle,' etc., but the personal, loving God who speaks to us and who says: 'I am the Lord your God' (Ex. 20). The God of Scripture is not a god defined by abstract thought but the God who defines himself as he discloses himself in personal encounter. *This affirmation is theological axiom.*"[15]

The revelation of God, therefore, as personal self-disclosure, is a relational event. Truth communicated between living beings always involves some sort of relationship—whether one of belief or disbelief, love or hate, action or passivity. Information by itself may move along a one-way street; *communication* of information, though, happens on a two-way street. Speaking doesn't necessarily infer hearing (as anyone who has tried to talk with someone absorbed in a book or television can attest), but speaking that becomes communication—a revelatory event—does infer a hearer who responds. The Word, because it is not simply ideas floating in abstraction but a concrete person who calls for a response of fellowship, unites us to God.

THE NECESSITY OF TRUST

The more personally revealing the communication, the more important the relationship. A woman may tell a man how to use a new computer program, and the dialogue will demand little in the way of personal interaction. But if they develop an interest in each other *as persons*, self-revelations will increase as mutual trust grows; if they fall in love and commit the ultimate self-exposure called marriage, they will do so, presumably, because of the deepest confidence in one another.

In a similar way, knowledge of God, because it is personal, becomes accessible to us in a relationship of trust. The Word comes *from* God and *to* us; we add nothing to it. But we are not completely passive. Because the Word is a person, Jesus Christ, we gain access to the divine disclosure in a relational manner. "To all who received him," John said, "who believed in his name, he gave power to become children of God" (John 1:12). To receive him, to believe in his name, to have faith—these phrases are nearly synonymous in the Bible to describe the entrusting of ourselves to One who embodies God's revelation, Jesus Christ.

Careful observation of anything demands that the manner of study be consistent with the object of study. Astronomers observe stars with a telescope, biologists examine cells with a microscope, sociologists discover patterns of human behavior with surveys and interviews, psychiatrists delve into the subconscious through in-depth conversation—and Christians becomes attentive to God's self-revelation by entrusting themselves to Jesus Christ.

St. Anselm described the theological enterprise as *fides quaerens intellectum*, "faith seeking understanding." It's a matter of first things first. We do not seek to understand in order to believe, but we believe in order to understand. "What we call our knowledge of Christ," Helmut Thielicke said, "is imparted to us only as we achieve a personal relation of trust in him."[16] If we seek to understand the God-Man in a non-relational way, simply as another piece of external knowledge, we will be overwhelmed by difficulties, by a host of paradoxical gymnastics: How can he be both divine and human? How can he be both exalted Lord and humble servant? Before long we will be lost in an intellectual maze. How different if we begin with faith! Jesus first said to his disciples, "Follow me." Only after a few years of journeying together did he dare ask them, "Who do you say that I am?" As we journey toward knowledge of God along a difficult, rocky road, we will be held by the hand of One whom we trust, One who we know transcends our thoughts and yet leads us to understanding.

FAITH BLIND TO ITSELF

As important as faith is, *the object of study is not our faith*. Faith that looks to itself is not faith—at least not in the biblical sense. We do not find God by looking deep within ourselves or by following our best instincts or by heeding our consciences or by listening to a "still small voice." Navel-gazing—even spiritual navel-gazing—reveals nothing but navels. To quote Freeman Patterson once more: "Letting go of self is an essential precondition to real seeing."[17] The great necessity is to get attention off ourselves and onto God. Faith, therefore, turns outward, away from itself toward Jesus Christ.

Before beginning doctoral work at Edinburgh University, I went to Scotland a few weeks in advance of my family in order to find housing. A few days after my arrival, having some time to myself, I attended a concert at Usher Hall. It was a delightful evening—until the performance concluded and I walked out into a very rainy night. I hadn't taken an umbrella; I hadn't even taken a raincoat. Not to worry, I assured myself, because I could run back to my room before I got too soaked. So with confidence bolstered by complete ignorance, I raced off through dark streets. The rain fell with increasing conviction, everything became more unfamiliar, and fear formed like a ball in my guts and rose, regardless of my efforts to keep it down, into my consciousness, gnawing at my courage. Eventually, as W. C. Fields put it, I had to take the bull by the tail and face the situation: I was outrageously lost. I needed help, but even muggers and stray cats had quit the night. I wandered aimlessly, despairingly.

A man appeared. What assignation had set him in such inhospitable circumstances? A tryst with his mistress? Or to find me? Do angels speak with a Scottish accent? Whoever he was, I needed him.

"Sir, can you tell me the way to Pollack Residence Halls?"

"Aye. You need to go three blocks down this street, and then turn left on Clerk, go for two blocks, and then turn right. . . ." He stopped when he saw the confusion in my eyes. "Och," he said, "I'll show you. Follow me."

In the moments that followed I had perhaps the purest form of faith I have ever experienced: I entrusted myself totally to this man's guidance. I dedicated not a fleeting second of thought to my watery appearance, my fearful panting, my confused speech—or my trust in this stranger. At the time, my faith seemed—and was!—completely unremarkable; my attention was devoted exclusively to my savior, to what he was saying and where he was going.

Authentic Christian faith is blind in this way. It is necessary for the knowledge of a personal God; only in trust do we receive the divine revelation given to us in Jesus Christ. But faith is as much aware of itself as a dazed lover is conscious of himself; it exists only in blissful ignorance of itself and passionate captivity to the beloved's charms. Faith's attention stays fixed on the object of its confidence.

The revelation of God, in other words, is objective, something that comes from outside history, from outside our thoughts and feelings; it stands over against us, speaking to us, judging us and saving us and transforming us. But this "something" is a person, Jesus Christ, and thus our necessary response is subjective, an act of trust in which we become open to the *personal* truth of God.

Our side of the relationship shouldn't much interest us, though, for whenever truant eyes look inward, they see abundant weakness and doubt. As Peter floundered in the Sea of Galilee by taking his eyes off the Master, we flounder in a deadly sea of subjectivity the moment we become fascinated with what we're doing; if we watch the wind and waves and our improbable walking, we sink faster than a cement block. Salvation—from ourselves and the pathetic gods of our own making—comes only by looking up and taking the hand of the One who can lift us into an understanding of God.

ENCOUNTERING JESUS CHRIST

When we grasp the hand of Jesus Christ, we meet God. But how does this happen? Where do we encounter Jesus Christ?

Surely not through an "inner light," for we have seen the mischief we can be led into by a religious subjectivity that too eagerly slips its leash to sniff about for back-alley experiences to satisfy its spiritual lusts. But under the porches of our little neighborhood, subjectivity never finds anything more than trivial gods, which, though perhaps cooling the heat of the moment, ultimately leave us wandering down paths of unfulfilled longing. Thank God, Jesus Christ comes to us from outside our experiences, from outside our pious achievements and intuitions and feelings.

Where, then, do we encounter Jesus Christ? Perhaps in history? No, not exactly, though many have attempted to find him there, trying by means of "objective" research to get behind the Bible in the "quest for the historical Jesus" (nineteenth century), and the "new quest for the historical Jesus" (mid-twentieth century), and most recently in the quests of John P. Meier,[18] John Dominic Crossan,[19] and the notorious "Jesus Seminar." But this approach is filled with difficulties, not the least of which is that we are dependent upon the New Testament Gospels—documents which, though certainly resting upon history, are not biographical in the modern sense of the word. The data come not from scholars endeavoring to stand apart from past events as neutral observers, but from believers, from witnesses to good news about a resurrected Savior who had seized them with the love of God. Any attempt to strip away the convictions of these witnesses to uncover a bare kernel of history will yield precious little, for as we have seen, Jesus Christ is encountered only in the relationship of faith. The first disciples met him in faith, and now through their faith we meet him with our own.

Jesus Christ is the eternal Word who became flesh and lived among us. The personal revelation of God became, in the words of the Chalcedon Creed, "at once complete in Godhead and complete in manhood, truly God and truly man." This act of humility continues, the Word becomes flesh again and again, through the testimony of Scripture. Stated another way, the Holy Spirit who dwelt fully in Jesus Christ and who inspired the apostolic witness to him now inspires our reading of it: through the dynamic work of the Spirit, God's Word meets us in something that is not dead but "living and active, sharper than any two-edged sword" (Hebrews 4:12).

We will think more about the role of Scripture as a conduit for the dynamic Word in chapter nine, but for now we must understand that we know God only through Jesus Christ, and we know Jesus Christ only through Scripture.

When we stay focused on the Jesus Christ we meet in the New Testament, we discover no "gentle Jesus, meek and mild," but One who grabs us by the scruff of the neck to shake loose from us all false images of deity we have cherished, One who is the Great Iconoclast smashing to bits our trivial gods.

How can we believe in the god-of-my-cause, if the living God is present in One who would not be co-opted by anyone's cause, One who was finally rejected by every group—Pharisees, Sadducees, Zealots, and Romans alike—because he didn't fit any of the "politically correct" orthodoxies of his day?

How can we believe in the god-of-my-understanding, if the living God is present in One who constantly confounded the wise and held up children as model candidates for the King-dom, One who taught in paradoxes and parables that still tease out questions in hearers and break open hard certainties with the hammer of enigma?

How can we believe in the god-of-my-experience, if the liv-ing God is present in One who dealt with individuals in unique ways, One who called a tax collector to himself but to another said, "Sell all that you own and distribute the money to the poor . . . then come, follow me," One who seemed to tolerate Peter's impulsiveness but cautioned other would-be disciples to "count the cost"?

How can we believe in the god-of-my-comfort, if the living God is present in One who said, "Foxes, and birds of the air have nests; but the Son of Man has nowhere to lay his head," One who warned, "If any want to become my followers, let them deny themselves and take up their cross and follow me"?

How can we believe in the god-of-my-success, if the living God is present in One who began his life on the lowest rung of society and ended it even lower, One who died despised and rejected, abandoned even by his erstwhile disciples?

How can we believe in the god-of-my-nation, if the living God is present in One who, when questioned at his trial, said plainly, "My kingdom is not from this world," One who has been worshiped as lord by followers from nearly every nation on earth?

We may be attracted or repelled by this Jesus Christ, we may be comforted or disturbed by him, we may follow him or run the other direction, but we must admit that if God is revealed in him, God is different—*fundamentally* different—from anything we could have imagined, from any god we might have created for ourselves. The biblical word for this dif-ference is *holy*.

CHAPTER SIX

Consuming Fire

A few days after Blaise Pascal's death in 1662, a servant happened to find hidden in the lining of his master's coat a little piece of parchment paper covered with the philosopher's own writing. For eight years Pascal had kept close to himself this testimony to a life-changing encounter:

In the year of Grace, 1654,
On Monday, 23rd of November, Feast of St. Clement,
Pope and Martyr, and of others in the Martyrology,
Vigil of Saint Chrysogonus, martyr and others,
From about half past ten in the evening
until about half past twelve
FIRE
God of Abraham, God of Isaac, God of Jacob
not of the philosophers and scholars.
Certitude. Certitude. Feeling. Joy. Peace.
God of Jesus Christ.

The FIRE that had consumed Pascal had nothing to do with the abstract deity of philosophers and scholars; it was the flame that singed Abraham, Isaac, and Jacob, the flame that blazed forth in Jesus Christ.

Who is God? Keeping our eyes fixed on Jesus Christ, the fundamental affirmation we must make is that *God is holy*. God is the consuming fire of holiness—a fire wholly other than creation and a fire burning with redeeming love for creation.

THE HOLY ONE OF HOLY GOD

Jesus Christ, the image of the invisible God, neither taught a new religion nor revealed a new God. He was a son of Israel, born into a family who worshiped and served the God who called Abraham, the God who delivered the law through Moses, the God who reigned through David, the God who spoke through Isaiah and Jeremiah and all the prophets—the God we meet, in other words, in the Old Testament, the One whom Isaiah saw in the Temple, with seraphs in attendance calling to one another, "Holy, holy, holy is the LORD of hosts," the One who said through Hosea, "I am God and no mortal, the Holy One in your midst."

Because *this* God sent Jesus as the fulfillment of centuries of history-making promises, and because God sent *this* Jesus to reveal the divine heart and to save the world, it should not be surprising that Jesus, according to Luke's account, was born through the power of the *Holy* Spirit. The angelic messenger said to Mary, "The child to be born will be holy; he will be called the Son of God." And when he began his ministry, even demonic powers witnessed to this, saying, "Let us alone! What have you to do with us, Jesus of Nazareth? . . . I know who you are, the Holy One of God." Simon Peter spoke for the rest of the disciples when he confessed, "We have come to believe and know that you are the Holy One of God."[1]

When Jesus taught his disciples to pray, he said the first petition to "our Father in heaven," should be "hallowed be your name." Our first concern, our deepest passion, should be that God hallow—reveal as holy, and cause to be revered as holy—the divine name. In the Bible, a "name is one's real, as opposed to one's supposed, identification; one's real identity or character as opposed to rumors or fabrications; one's revealed nature as opposed to one's surmised."[2] So to pray for the hallowing of God's name is to petition God to be God, to break forth in revelation as the Holy One in our midst. This, Jesus said, should be at the top of our prayer list.

The God revealed in Jesus Christ is holy. But what does this mean? What is holiness?

THE GREAT STRANGER

Insofar as the meaning of "holy" can be determined etymologically, the word originally had reference to *"that which is marked off, withdrawn from ordinary use."*[3] As von Rad stated it, "the holy could much more aptly be designated the great stranger in the human world, that is, a datum of experience which can never really be co-ordinated into the world in which man is at home, and over against which he initially feels fear rather than trust—it is, in fact, the 'wholly other.'"[4] Holiness, then, is something utterly distinct, "the great stranger."

In the life and faith of Israel the term *holiness* underwent significant development. Two major streams of tradition have been noted which, though overlapping, are distinctly discernible in the Old Testament: the *religious* and the *ethical*.[5]

The earliest stream of biblical literature links holiness with what scholars designate "the cult"—a term referring to Israel's system of religious rites. The word *holiness* cannot be found in Genesis, where the cult plays no significant role, but it does emerge in Exodus with the story of Moses. It denotes not an action but a state, as shown in the fact that objects are considered holy—the ground around the burning bush, Jerusalem, the site of the Temple, the Temple itself, the "holiest of holies."[6] In Leviticus we read of holy offerings, the "most holy" guilt offering, holy linen, the holy place of the atonement, holy convocations, the holy tithe of the land, and so on.[7]

Holiness in the cult, however, is not limited to a materialistic understanding. In fact, an important development takes place: the word *holy* becomes associated with persons. As a predicate of God it undergoes personalization until it fuses with divinity so completely that finally Yahweh's holiness contrasts with everything creaturely.

In its most primitive use, then, holiness has to do with that which is separate. First, as applied to the cult, it refers to things set apart for God's service; second, as applied to the name and person of God, it emphasizes the utter uniqueness of God. Thus the Holy is first a *religious,* not an ethical, term, indicating something alien to ordinary human life: either things set apart by God or the personal being of God.

ETHICAL PURITY

An important development eventually takes place in the biblical literature: an *ethical* dimension gets added to holiness. Because God has set apart not only objects but a people as well, the idea of a holy people emerges—a people who live according to a unique standard of conduct. The so-called Holiness Code of Leviticus rests on the statement, "You shall be holy, for I the LORD your God am holy" (19:2).

This ethical character of the Holy reaches full bloom in God's revelation through the prophets. The prophets angrily blast empty cultic ritualism and call the people of God to live justly by correcting oppression, defending the fatherless, and pleading for the widow. Perhaps this emphasis on conduct comes from a new appreciation of the moral distinctives of a holy God.

Hosea, especially, recasts the idea of the Holy in a new form.[8] Because God's holiness opposes the uncleanness of Israel, it has a death-dealing aspect that causes the final "stumbling" of Israel; yet holiness also has a creative element that makes God a tree of life. In a way that is astonishing in the context of Israel's religious tradition, Hosea links holiness and love. The holiness of Yahweh is precisely the creative love that heals as it tears and brings life through its slaying: "There can be no playing down the annihilating power of holiness, and the intensity of the threat of judgment in Hosea can hardly be exaggerated. Nevertheless, in the end it is *the incomprehensible creative power of love which marks out Yahweh as the wholly 'other,'* the one whose nature is in complete contrast to that of the created cosmos."[9] As Procksch summed up Hosea's view, "the antithe-

sis between God and man consists in the very love which over-
comes it."[10]

Isaiah develops further the image of the Holy One of Israel,
filling the phrase with a content not unlike Hosea's theology
of holiness. This prophet of the Exile focuses on the coming
deliverance. The Holy One is the Redeemer.[11] "A connection is
here established between salvation and holiness."[12] Yahweh's
holy "otherness" is revealed precisely in the power to save.

THE BLAZING UNION

This survey of the Old Testament understanding of holiness
reveals two important dimensions. First, a religious use of the
word *holy*, quite independent from moral connotations, was
woven into the fabric of Israel's cultic life. Here the word carried its most primitive etymological meaning: it signified the
"wholly other," the utterly separate. It was as readily applied
to things as to persons. It indicated the complete distinction
between the sacred and the profane.

But as the word *holy* became associated with the God of
Israel, it became more personalized—and the consequence
was an equation of holiness and deity. As Israel's God was
revealed more fully, the concept of holiness progressed accordingly. As God acted on behalf of the people, proving to be their
redeemer, this attribute became, by association, a defining characteristic of holiness. Thus an ethical dimension was united
with the religious.

So the Old Testament view of God's holiness may be summarized this way: God is utterly distinct, and this set-apartness
consists in the fact that God redeems, that God loves. Holiness,
therefore, refers to the fact that God is antithetical to humanity
precisely in the overcoming of the antithesis. The consuming
fire of holiness is a bonfire of love set to burning against the
world's night.

This union of the religious and ethical dimensions of holiness blazes into fulfillment in Jesus Christ—the One through
whom God reveals a separateness precisely in a gracious commitment *not* to be separate, the One through whom the otherness of God becomes a conflagration against sin, but with

flames that ignite an incandescence of truth in our darkness, that warm our lonely coldness, that kindle a fire of love in our own hearts. The saving grace of God in Jesus Christ sets a clear boundary between God and humanity; it moves along a one-way street, coming from God and accomplished in the power of God, as it judges the world's sin. And yet this judgment draws an inclusive boundary around a new relationship between God and humanity; it destroys the alienating power of sin by nailing it to the cross and opens the door to new life through the empty tomb. The holiness of God—wholly *other* as it is wholly *for*—separates and unites, judges and saves.

What God has joined together, however, theologians have split asunder. As their attention has wandered from Jesus Christ to abstract, speculative theories, they have allowed the idea of holiness once again to break apart into religious and ethical aspects.

HOLINESS AS *MYSTERIUM TREMENDUM*

Any discussion of God as "wholly other" can hardly avoid Rudolf Otto's influential book *The Idea of the Holy*, one of the most widely read theological works of the twentieth century. In setting out to observe the common characteristics of religious feeling in the presence of transcendence, Otto provides an experiential understanding of holiness.

In describing the ineffable character of the Holy, Otto introduces a term coined from the Latin *numen*, "the numinous." This is the object outside the perceiving mind that causes the "creature feeling" to arise within, "the note of submergence into nothingness before an overpowering, absolute might of some kind."[13]

The numinous has two sides to it. On the one hand, it is the *mysterium tremendum*, the element of daunting awfulness, majesty, that which evokes awe and terror in a person—the "wholly other."[14] On the other hand, there is something attractive, fascinating, about the numinous; it has a magnetic appeal. Otto calls this characteristic the *fascinans*. "These two qualities, the daunting and the fascinating, now combine in a strange harmony of contrasts,"[15] together representing the content of the Holy.

L. M. Montgomery's novel *Emily of New Moon* has a passage that conveys something of Otto's sense of the numinous:

> It had always seemed to Emily, ever since she could remember, that she was very, very near to a world of wonderful beauty. Between it and herself hung only a thin curtain; she could never draw the curtain aside—but sometimes, just for a moment, a wind fluttered it and then it was as if she caught a glimpse of the enchanting realm beyond—only a glimpse—and heard the note of unearthly music.
>
> This moment came rarely—went swiftly, leaving her breathless with the inexpressible delight of it. She could never recall it—never summon it—never pretend it; but the wonder of it stayed with her for days. It never came twice with the same thing. Tonight the dark boughs against that far off sky had given it. It had come with a high, wild note of wind in the night, with a shadow wave over a ripe field, with a gray bird lighting on her window-sill in a storm, with the singing of "Holy! Holy! Holy!" in church, with the glimpse of the kitchen fire when she had come home on a dark autumn night, with the spirit-like blue of ice palms on a twilight pane, with a felicitous new word when she was writing down a "description" of something. And always when the flash came to her Emily felt that life was a wonderful, mysterious thing of persistent beauty.[16]

Otto rediscovered the religious nature of the Holy, as distinct from the ethical, and he gave expression to feelings of awe-in-the-presence-of-mystery that most people experience at some time in their lives. But for Christian faith the Holy is not an empty, independent category; it knows only the Holy One of Israel revealed in the Holy One of Nazareth. True, there is always the "wholly other" dimension of holiness in biblical faith. But the separateness is "filled in" with a specific content: the "otherness" of God is precisely redemptive love. Abraham

Heschel, a Jewish theologian, identifies what is missing in Otto's approach: "The God of the prophets is not the wholly other, a strange, weird, uncanny Being, shrouded in unfathomable darkness, but the God of the covenant, whose will they know and are called upon to convey. The God they proclaim is not the Remote One, but the One who is invoked, near, and concerned."[17]

HOLINESS AS CLEANLINESS

Other theologians have stressed the *ethical* character of holiness. Paul Tillich attributes the association of the Holy with the morally clean to the influence of Calvin and his followers: "An almost neurotic anxiety about the unclean develops in later Calvinism. The word 'Puritan' is most indicative of this trend. The holy is the clean; cleanliness becomes holiness. This means the end of the numinous character of the holy. The *tremendum fascinosum* becomes pride of self-control and repression."[18]

A glance at Heinrich Heppe's *Reformed Dogmatics* would confirm that some Calvinists have indeed moved in the direction indicated by Tillich,[19] but a survey of standard dogmatic works shows that the description of holiness in moral categories wanders freely across theological lines.[20] In any event, the Holy *has* often been linked to notions of ethical purity. Thus Clarke writes, "the doctrine of holiness is at the deepest a doctrine of absolute and perfect moral excellence."[21]

Certainly this understanding of holiness coincides with *part* of the biblical witness. Moral cleanliness is connected with the Holy in both priestly and prophetic literature.

But this emphasis, as I have shown, is never purchased at the price of the religious dimension; the "wholly other" aspect never dissolves—not even in prophetic theology. Isaiah was overwhelmed with his own uncleanness in the presence of awesome majesty describable only in the symbolic language of royalty ("upon a throne, high and lifted up . . . his train filled the temple"), angelic beings ("above him stood the seraphim"), and cataclysmic violence ("the foundations of the thresholds shook"). The "woe is me!" of personal imperfection came from being in the presence of the "wholly other."[22]

UNITED IN CHRIST

Stressing either a purely religious or a purely ethical conception of holiness leads to a definition of God abstracted from the full, concrete revelation of God in Jesus Christ.

Otto's *mysterium tremendum* was discovered by means of empirical observation of the nature of religious experience in the presence of the "wholly other." The Holy, for him, is a general category distinct from any of its specific manifestations in human history. Jesus Christ has significance for Otto because he instantiates and fills out a previously determined—hence independent—category of holiness. But if Jesus Christ is the Word of God incarnate, the fullest and final self-revelation of God to humanity, all descriptions of God must begin with Jesus rather than with human experience.

Similarly, a one-sided emphasis on the ethical dimension of holiness is equally unacceptable, for it also leads away from the revelation in Christ toward abstract speculation. If we define God only by such terms as "cleanliness," "stainless purity," "moral goodness," and others taken from the realm of *human* values, do we not risk reducing God to our limited understanding of these terms, and thus create a god in our own image, after our own likeness, however many words we might employ to push this god into the heavens?

Because God has provided a trustworthy self-revelation in Jesus Christ, we should look nowhere else for our understanding of holiness. In Christ we see the uniting of the *complete otherness* shown in the original religious use of the word and the *mercy* revealed in the ethical application of the word. In this divine human and human deity, the distinction between God and humanity is not dissolved but paradoxically asserted precisely in overcoming the separation between them.

Because God in Jesus Christ donned the humble clothing of human flesh, gladly bearing our weaknesses and suffering, assuming full responsibility for our selfish rebellion, and finally defeating the power of death itself—because God has done all this for us, we describe this one-way movement from heaven to earth by one word: *grace*. Everything we know of God and everything we enjoy before God—forgiveness, access through prayer, appointment to service, eternal life—comes *from* God *to* us. Grace indicates a Giver with outstretched hands to receivers, a Superior in relation to inferiors; God remains God, we remain not-God. Grace keeps the boundary firmly in place. But because *grace* keeps the boundary in place, the distinctness is not distance; it is really a love who seeks a beloved, who summons to fellowship.

In *The Lion, the Witch, and the Wardrobe* C. S. Lewis describes the first time the children hear about Aslan:

> "Is—is he a man?" asked Lucy.
>
> "Aslan a man!" said Mr. Beaver sternly. "Certainly not. I tell you he is the King of the wood and the son of the great Emperor-Beyond-the-Sea. Don't you know who is the King of the Beasts? Aslan is a lion—*the* Lion, the great Lion."
>
> "Ooh!" said Susan. "I'd thought he was a man. Is he—quite safe? I shall feel rather nervous about meeting a lion."
>
> "That you will, dearie, and no mistake," said Mrs. Beaver. "If there's anyone who can appear before Aslan without their knees knocking, they're either braver than most or else just silly."
>
> "Then he isn't safe?" said Lucy.
>
> "Safe?" said Mr. Beaver. "Don't you hear what Mrs. Beaver tells you? Who said anything about safe? 'Course he isn't safe. But he's good. He's the King, I tell you."[23]

Like Aslan, God is definitely not safe. To appear before the Wholly Other with steady knees—well, it would be foolhardy, to say the least. In the presence of this One, human indifference gets slapped to alert attention and human pretension gets knocked on its backside. One may appear before other gods with confidence, with no sense of being threatened. They will stay put; they don't stray from places assigned to them by human egos desperately trying to maintain control. But the God revealed in Jesus Christ is holy, and a holy God cannot be contained or tamed. This sort of God is wholly other.

God is not safe, but God is good, very good. For the dangerous otherness is a transcendent, loving commitment not to be separate—a threat to our egos that establishes our true selves, a danger that is our only safety.

"Our God is a consuming fire." As children we were told not to play with matches, and as adults we treat fire with caution. We must. Fire demands respect for its regal estate: it will not be touched, it will be approached with care, and it wields its scepter for ill or for good. With one spark it can condemn a forest to ashes and a home to memory as ghostly as the smoke rising from the charred remains of the family album. Or with a single flame it can crown a candle with power to warm a romance and set to dancing a fireplace blaze that defends against the cold. Fire is dangerous, to be sure, but we cannot live without it; fire destroys but also sustains life.

The blaze of holiness admits no disrespect; its boundaries cannot be trespassed. But this very distinctness is the fire that thaws our frozen hearts, the fire that draws us into relationship with God and one another, the fire that cleanses even as it purges.

CHAPTER SEVEN

Conversion into Community

The cleansing fire of holiness reveals something important about us: we are loved sinners. In the blazing light of God's grace, we discover our true identity. We are those who *need* grace, who need a love that delivers and forgives and restores.

At the beginning of his *Institutes of the Christian Religion* John Calvin declared, "Without the knowledge of God there is no knowledge of self . . . it is certain that man never achieves a clear knowledge of himself unless he has first looked upon God's face, and then descends from contemplating him to scrutinize himself." Calvin went on to illustrate:

> For if in broad daylight we either look down upon the
> ground or survey whatever meets our view round
> about, we seem to ourselves endowed with the strongest
> and keenest sight; yet when we look up to the sun and
> gaze straight at it, that power of sight which was partic-
> ularly strong on earth is at once blunted and confused
> by a great brilliance, and thus we are compelled to admit
> that our keenness in looking upon things earthly is sheer

dullness when it comes to the sun. So it happens in esti-
mating our spiritual goods. . . . Then, what masquerad-
ing earlier as righteousness was pleasing in us will soon
grow filthy in its consummate wickedness. What wonderfully impressed us under the name of wisdom will
stink in its very foolishness. What wore the face of
power will prove itself the most miserable weakness.
That is, what in us seems perfection itself corresponds
ill to the purity of God.[1]

A WORLD GONE AWRY

Calvin's language seems strange to us. The syntax of sin is
unfamiliar; phrases like "consummate wickedness" sound like
a foreign language. A few years ago *The Wall Street Journal*
placed an advertisement in the *New York Times*, which was a
reprint of a provocative editorial that had appeared in the *Journal*. It recounted the moral confusions of the Clarence Thomas
hearings, the William Kennedy Smith affair, high-school sex,
an addicted culture, and so on:

> Sin isn't something that many people, including most
> churches, have spent much time talking about or worry-
> ing about through the years of the [cultural and sexual]
> revolution. But we will say this for sin; it at least offered
> a frame of reference for personal behavior. When the
> frame was dismantled, guilt wasn't the only thing that
> fell away; we also lost the guidewire of personal respon-
> sibility. . . . Everyone was left on his or her own. It now
> appears that many wrecked people could have used a
> road map. . . . Ministers and priests gave way (voluntar-
> ily) to clinics and counselors. Instead of giving your kid
> a dressing-down, you now give him (or her) a condom.
> The ministers of the therapeutic say the dressing-down
> is useless because the kids don't know what you're talk-
> ing about anyway. By now, they may be right.[2]

Talking about sin may be bad form, but even so, we know
things aren't right; we know something is wrong. The movie

Grand Canyon tells the story of an immigration attorney who attempts a short cut around a traffic jam. His bypass takes him along streets that seem progressively darker and more threatening. Then the nightmare begins: his fancy sports car stalls on one of those streets whose inhabitants wear guns and sneakers. He manages to telephone for a tow truck, but before it arrives, five young toughs surround and threaten him. The tow truck appears just in time, and its driver begins to hook up the sports car. The gang members protest; they had other plans. So the driver takes the group leader aside and says, "Man, the world ain't s'pposed to work like this. Maybe you don't know that, but this ain't the way it's s'pposed to be. I'm s'pposed to be able to do my job without askin' you if I can. And that dude is s'pposed to be able to wait with his car without you rippin' him off. Everything's s'pposed to be different than what it is here."[3]

The truck driver was right: the world ain't s'pposed to work like this. What has happened? Human beings, though created in the image of God and thus created for love, have turned away from their God-appointed orientation and have become *un*holy. God's holiness, as I argued in the last chapter, is precisely the distinction that bridges separation, the love that seeks fellowship. Human sin, conversely, is the opposite: not hate exactly but a profound self-absorption.

Donald Baillie provides a memorable image of what has gone wrong, "a tale of God calling His human children to form a great circle for the playing of His game":

> In that circle we ought all to be standing, linked together with lovingly joined hands, facing towards the Light in the centre, which is God ("the Love that moves the sun and the other stars"); seeing our fellow creatures all round the circle in the light of that central Love, which shines on them and beautifies their faces; and joining with them in the dance of God's great game, the rhythm of love universal. But instead of that, we have, each one, turned our backs upon God and the circle of our fellows, and faced the other way, so that we can see neither the Light at the centre nor the faces on the circumference. And indeed in that position it is difficult

even to join hands with our fellows! Therefore instead of playing God's game we play, each one, our own selfish little game. . . . Each one of us wishes to be the centre, and there is blind confusion, and not even any true *knowledge* of God or of our neighbours. That is what is wrong. . . .[4]

DANCE OF DEATH

Let's take the image a step further: the Light at the center is the Creator, the fount of life. To turn away from this, therefore, is to turn toward its opposite, toward death. The darkness in which we do our bounce and shimmy of desperation is "the valley of the shadow of death." We walk through this valley, not just when we take our last gasps through rubber tubes in the intensive care unit, but from our first gulps of air, still wet from our mother's womb. Throughout our lives we journey in a darkness only occasionally pierced by shafts of light promising the dawn of a different order; for the most part it is an unrelenting darkness, a darkness that aggressively reaches its cold fingers into every corner of our lives, touching us with intimations of more to come as we cough and sneeze or grasping us in all its horror as a child takes her last breath in our arms or we kiss the icy brow of a beloved lying stiff as a sentinel in a coffin.

In her novel *The Living*, Annie Dillard describes this scene:

> Hugh stood with stiff Lulu and supple Bert at the graveside. The Nooksacks stood together with their preacher. Before the funeral, in mourning for his father, they had shrieked and pounded on boards. . . .
> At last big-faced Norval Tawes read Scripture and prayed. "O Death, where is thy sting?" Norval Tawes called out, and his little black eyes glittered on Hugh.
> Hugh thought, *Just about everywhere, since you ask.*[5]

The lament of the apostle Paul may well serve as a cry for us all: "Wretched one that I am! Who will rescue me from this body of death?" Or perhaps we should ask, Who *can* rescue me from this body of death? Who can deliver me from the shadows and turn me toward the Light? Who can turn us all around so that we join hands once more and start a new dance, a dance of life?

PURGING FIRE

The apostle's answer came hard on his question: "Thanks be to God through Jesus Christ our Lord!" Which is to say, the impossible has been made possible through God's act of salvation in Jesus Christ. No trivial god could have accomplished this; it takes holiness for something this big, holiness to reconcile all things, from the individual soul to the farthest reaches of the cosmos.

Only a wholly other God *could* save, and only a God wholly other in self-giving love *would* save. Only a God different from humanity, outside the world of self-centeredness, has the power to reverse the deadly order of things. And only a God whose difference is the passion not to be separate—yes, the *passion*, the suffering—would go to the extremes necessary to cancel sin and put death itself to death.

The fire of holiness, as it burns against unholiness, first purges. The grace of God's commitment not to be separate includes the judgment of God's opposition against all that creates the separation.

Judgment is not a popular notion today—especially the thought of *God's* judgment. We prefer to imagine a deity who happily lets bygones be bygones, who winks at failures and pats us on the back to build our self-esteem. But according to Scripture, "God is love." And love devoid of judgment is only watered-down kindness.

The holy God is not "kind." Love is something far more stern and splendid than mere kindness. As C. S. Lewis put it,

> Kindness . . . cares not whether its object becomes good or bad, provided only that it escapes suffering. As Scripture points out, it is bastards who are spoiled: the legitimate sons, who are to carry on the family tradition, are punished. It is for people whom we care nothing about that we demand happiness on any terms: with our

friends, our lovers, our children, we are exacting and
would rather see them suffer much than be happy in
contemptible and estranging modes. If God is Love, He
is, by definition, something more than mere kindness.
And it appears, from all records, that though He has
often rebuked us and condemned us, He has never
regarded us with contempt. He has paid us the intolera-
ble compliment of loving us, in the deepest, most tragic,
most inexorable sense.[6]

Father Zossima, a character in Dostoyevsky's *The Brothers
Karamazov*, comments, "Love in action is a harsh and dreadful
thing, compared with love in dreams." The real thing wants
the best for the beloved, and that may mean a mother denying
her child's insistent plea for more candy, or a social worker
holding his client responsible for destructive behavior, or a wife
demanding a change in the behavior of her abusive husband—
or God damning to hell the sin that is destroying creation.

Which is precisely what has happened. The *Yes* toward
humanity flowing from the holiness of God includes a *No*
toward the self-centeredness destroying humanity; grace
includes judgment. This *Yes* and *No*—this grace and judgment
of God—have been fulfilled in Jesus Christ. The One in whom
"all the fullness of God was pleased to dwell" is the same One
through whom "God was pleased to reconcile to himself all
things, whether on earth or in heaven, by making peace
through the blood of his cross" (Colossians 1:19-20).

How did "the blood of his cross" make peace? Imagine a
courtroom scene in which the accused has been convicted of a
heinous crime. The judge, upholding the law and honoring the
demands of justice, declares the sentence of death. But then—
and here imagination necessarily founders against the rock of
plausibility—the judge announces that he himself will take the
place of the condemned, that he himself will bear the burden
and responsibility of guilt, that he himself will die. The truth
of the criminal's wrongdoing will not be ignored, but through
a sacrificial offering it will be atoned.

As difficult as this is to imagine, it is what Scripture says
happened in Jesus Christ. The One in whom the fullness of

God was pleased to dwell was the One by whom the fullness of sin was put to death. The Son of God took upon himself—and thus took into the being of God—the just consequences of humanity's turning from the Light. The absolute darkness we so richly deserve, the death that is essentially separation from God, was accepted on our behalf by the One who cried out with his last breath, "My God, my God, why have you forsaken me?"

Charles Colson tells of visiting a prison in the city of Sao Jose dos Campos, one that was turned over to two Christians twenty years ago:

> They called it Humaita, and their plan was to run it on Christian principles. The prison has only two full-time staff; the rest of the work is done by inmates. Every prisoner is assigned another inmate to whom he is accountable. In addition, every prisoner is assigned a volunteer family from the outside that works with him during his term and after his release. Every prisoner joins a chapel program, or else takes a course in character formation.
>
> When I visited Humaita, I found the inmates smiling—particularly the murderer who held the keys, opened the gates, and let me in. Wherever I walked I saw men at peace. I saw clean living areas, people working industriously. The walls were decorated with biblical sayings from Psalms and Proverbs. Humaita has an astonishing record. Its recidivism rate is 4 percent compared to 75 percent in the rest of Brazil and the United States. How is all this possible?
>
> I saw the answer when my guide escorted me to the notorious punishment cell once used for torture. Today, he told me, that block houses only a single inmate. As we reached the end of a long concrete corridor and he put the key into the lock, he paused and asked, "Are you sure you want to go in?"
>
> "Of course," I replied impatiently. "I've been in isolation cells all over the world." Slowly he swung open the massive door, and I saw the prisoner in that punishment

cell: a crucifix, beautifully carved by the Humaita
inmates—the prisoner Jesus hanging on the cross.

"He's doing time for all the rest of us," my guide
said softly.[7]

The Judge took the place of the condemned, the Holy One
did time for all the rest of us so that we can be set free from the
prison of death. Holiness, therefore, is not a passive state of
being; holiness is an active fire of salvation. The wholly other
God took an eternal stand against disobedient self-centeredness, blazing forth against sin. And yet, because God is wholly
other in love, the flames of judgment leapt out of an overflowing cauldron of mercy. God's absolute separateness is revealed
most clearly in the place where that separation is bridged.

THE TURN-AROUND

The central witness of the New Testament is this: the One
crucified on a cross was raised from the tomb, the One put to
death for the sake of sin was resurrected for the sake of life—
for the sake of God's life over against death, as a final *Yes* tri-
umphing over the real but only penultimate *No*, as a promise
of a great turn-around in which the dance begins anew. "Christ
has been raised from the dead," Paul told the Christians at
Corinth, "the first fruits of those who have died. For since
death came through a human being, the resurrection of the
dead has also come through a human being; for as all die in
Adam, so all will be made alive in Christ" (1 Corinthians
15:20-22). And Paul summarized the consequence in a later
letter to the same congregation: "So if anyone is in Christ, there
is a new creation: everything old has passed away; see, everything has become new! All this is from God, who reconciled us
to himself through Christ" (2 Corinthians 5:17-18).

All this is from God. The restoration of creation is God's
work from beginning to end. The turn-around happens not
because God started it and left us to finish it by cranking up
enough good intentions and spiritual resolve to turn on the
heels of sin toward the Light. It happens because God who is
the sending Father and the sent Son is also the indwelling Holy

Spirit, who beams the transforming Light within us, melting down our cold resistance and warming our hearts until we desire nothing so much as to turn toward the Source at the center. God's Spirit—the *Holy* Spirit—completes the work of holiness, transforming us "from one degree of glory to another" (2 Corinthians 3:18). As David Hubbard expressed it, "In a massive conspiracy of grace Father, Son, and Spirit have plotted together to turn our lives around."[8]

Grace means that God does for us and in us what we cannot do for ourselves; grace means that salvation is a gift. Robert Capon asks:

> Do you now see what you have to do to be saved? Do you at last understand the precise degree of cooperation on your part needed to enable you to enter into life? Do you finally recognize that all that is required of you is to do exactly what Lazarus did—which is exactly and only *nothing*? Martha spoke the whole truth, not only about Lazarus, but about everyone of us in particular and about the human race in general: "Lord, by now we stink." We have been dead 4 days, 4,000 days, 400,000 times 4,000 days. In the midst of all our life we have been in death. And in the midst of that abiding death we have been in Nothing. Knee-deep in it, waist-deep in it, up to our noses, and in over our heads in Not-a-Thing. But now in Lazarus, you see it is just that extremity that has always been our hope, that very prison, the doorway to our liberty. Because making things jump out of nothing is God's favorite act. He creates us out of it and he raises us up from it. Jesus came to raise the dead. Not to improve the improvable, not to perfect the perfectible, but to raise the dead. He never met a corpse that didn't sit right up then and there. And he never meets us without bringing us out of nothing into the joy of his resurrection: you, me, the President of the United States and poor old Arthur down by the docks with his pint of Muscatel in a brown paper bag. We are all dead. And he raises us all. And without so much as a by-your-leave. Just be a good corpse and he does the rest.

Because his Word is the Word with the ultimate bark
and when he says, "Arthur, come forth," that's all old
Arthur needs. His nuthin' ain't nuthin no more.[9]

CAPITULATION

To call this grace "good news"—gospel—is true enough, but
we should understand that ordinary words really can't bear
the full burden of meaning. The weight of joy puts a severe
strain on our language. Fantasy writer J. R. R. Tolkien invented
a new word for situations like this: *eucatastrophe*—a good
upheaval, a wonderful convulsion. A scene from *The Lord of the
Rings* expresses it well:

> "Gandalf! [Sam said] I thought you were dead! But then
> I thought I was dead myself. Is everything sad going to
> come untrue? What's happened to the world?"
>
> "A great Shadow has departed," said Gandalf, and
> then he laughed, and the sound was like music, or like
> water in a parched land; and as he listened the thought
> came to Sam that he had not heard laugher, the pure
> sound of merriment, for days upon days without count.
> It fell upon his ears like the echo of all the joys he had
> ever known. But he himself burst into tears. Then, as a
> sweet rain will pass down a wind of spring and the sun
> will shine out the clearer, his tears ceased, and his laugh-
> ter welled up, and laughing he sprang from his bed.
>
> "How do I feel?" he cried. "Well, I don't know how
> to say it. I feel, I feel"—he waved his arms in the air—
> "I feel like spring after winter, and sun on the leaves;
> and like trumpets and harps and all the songs I have
> ever heard!"[10]

The New Testament uses different words—salvation,
redemption, reconciliation, resurrection, glory—to describe different aspects of God's work in Christ, but they all point to the
Great Eucatastrophe, the victorious eruption of God's holiness
in a world of sin. They ask us to listen to what Dante heard at
the end of his long ascent from hell to heaven: a sound like the

laughter of the universe. It is the laughter of holiness, as lamentation breaks into jubilation, as despair gives way to hope, as a world long frozen in sin cracks open to Life.

What can we do but join the laughter? To laugh is to surrender, to capitulate to a surprising incongruity. Think of the stuff of which humor is made: a silly story about St. Peter at the Pearly Gates ends with an unexpected punch line; a preacher proceeds down the aisle gloriously oblivious to a strand of toilet paper caught in his belt and streaming behind him like a vestment of embarrassment; a two-year-old decides a bowl would make a wonderful hat but doesn't bother to empty the spaghetti before putting it on her head; Charlie Chaplin slips on a banana peel—and we can't help but laugh. Laughter is a happy release of the tension created by an unexpected turn of events.

And the grandest surprise of all, the greatest reversal ever, has happened by God's grace in Jesus Christ. Who could have guessed it? What can we do but surrender to it? Our response is like laughter, but we should now use the biblical word for it: faith. Faith is not a work we do to complete God's work of salvation; it's not something for which we can pat ourselves on the back. Faith throws down the arms of rebellious resistance and gives in to the way things really are, and that means gives in to God. Faith, quite simply, is trust. To have faith is to entrust oneself to the goodness of a holy God whose love has been so clearly revealed in Jesus Christ. "Faith," Helmut Thielicke said, "can be described only as a movement of flight, flight away from myself and toward the great possibilities of God."[11]

FROM SELF TO A NEW COMMUNITY

A consequence of faith is the disestablishment of the false, autonomous self. When I entrust myself to God, when I turn around and face the Light at the center, I lose my disobedient ego-centricity; but I gain the self I was created to be. I become a person-in-community, a person in fellowship with God and others. Emil Brunner has aptly described this change:

> That is faith: a change of hands, a revolution, an overthrow of government. A lord of self becomes one who

obeys. . . . Solitariness is now also past. The imperious,
reserved "I" is broken open; into my world, in which I
was alone . . . into the solitariness of the "Thou-less" I,
God has stepped as Thou. He who believes is never solitary. Faith is the radical overcoming of the I-solitariness.
The monologue of existence—even that existence in
which many things have been talked about with many
people—has become the dialogue of existence: now
there is unconditional fellowship.[12]

This unconditional fellowship is, first of all, between God
and the one who has capitulated in faith. On the basis of the
justice and mercy in Christ's work of salvation, God forgives
sin. *Absolute* forgiveness for *all* sin. This is an important part of
the eucatastrophe, for though we may have lost a conscious
awareness of sin and the language to speak about it, we have
not lost feelings of guilt. Something within us witnesses to a
fundamental disorder; we have a nagging sense that things are
not right and that somehow we are to blame.

Ernest Hemingway once told a story to illustrate the popularity of the Spanish name Paco. A father, he said, journeyed
to Madrid to put an ad in the local paper: PACO MEET ME AT
HOTEL MONTANA NOON WEDNESDAY ALL IS FORGIVEN PAPA. The
next day the authorities had to muster a squadron of the
Guardia Civil to disperse the mob of 800 young men who
massed on the street in front of the inn.[13]

So we stand: at the front door of the inn, hoping against
hope that we are forgiven. And the Word of the Gospel tells us
that yes, we are called by a Father who has been waiting for
our return and now bids us come in and be seated at the banquet table. A ring is placed on our fingers and robes around our
shoulders and sandals on our feet. The fatted calf is killed, the
musicians are cutting loose, and the guests are getting down
with some serious dancing.

The guests? We suddenly realize that all the other Pacos
have also been invited, that the Father has welcomed every
prodigal home from the far country. Before we quite know
what has happened we're on our feet, moving to the rhythm
of grace. Someone has grasped our right hand, someone else

our left. A great circle has been formed, it seems, around the Father at the center, and the Father's love is so real, so intensely palpable, it's like light—pure, primordial Light—shining forth with transforming luminosity. We are able, for the first time, to see not only ourselves but one another.

A new community has been formed by the gracious invasion of God's holiness. Where there is loss of awe, God calls forth worship; where there is impatience with silence, God speaks forth the Word; where there is rampant individualism, God brings forth love. To each of these we now turn.

CHAPTER EIGHT

Community
of Worship

A few years ago my wife and I were invited to hear the great tenor Luciano Pavarotti. We were told the performance would likely be his last appearance on the west coast, and so we gratefully accepted the outrageously expensive tickets for two of the best seats in the house.

The concert exceeded our expectations. We were stunned by the master's music. In aria after aria he demonstrated remarkable talent—talent, surely, that set him apart from the thousands who had come to hear him. But that set-apartness was revealed in his generous giving; his uniqueness was shown in a gracious offering of himself. He held nothing back, it seemed. Every single note was filled with boundless passion and glorious beauty.

We *had* to respond: we jumped to our feet and clapped, hooted, and whistled. We did not stop, not for a long time. Wave after wave of grateful applause was sent up to the platform, calling forth encore after encore.

In the midst of this mayhem of gratitude, when my hands were beginning to ache from the pounding, I thought to myself, *This is deeply satisfying, a profound joy.* It felt right to offer praise in response to such excellence, and this sense of appropriateness created a congruence in which my little world, at least for the moment, seemed perfectly ordered.

In a similar way, God's gracious self-giving in Jesus Christ calls for the response of faith, and faith's first expression will be the applause of praise. Worship—the word comes from middle English, meaning to ascribe worth—is both an instinctive response and an inexhaustible source of joy.

THE RESPONSE OF JOY

Grace evokes gratitude, and a thankful heart needs to express itself. Nineteenth century English writer Harriet Martineau was something of an atheist. One day, reveling in the beauties of an autumn morning, she burst out, "Oh, I'm so grateful!"— to which her believing companion replied, "Grateful to whom, my dear?"[1] Gratitude needs someone to thank, and once gratitude discovers the ultimate Someone behind all good gifts, the Giver who has embraced us in eternal love, praise will follow, in Peter Marshall's words, "as the needle seeks the pole . . . as the sunflower seeks the sun . . . as the river seeks the sea . . . as the eagle seeks the ceiling of the world."

Brennan Manning refers to a scene from *Gideon*, a play written by a Brooklyn Jew named Paddy Chayefsky:

> Gideon is out in the desert in his tent a thousand miles from nowhere, feeling deserted and rejected by God. One night, God breaks into the tent and Gideon is seduced, ravished, over-come, burnt by the wild fire of God's love. He is up all night, pacing back and forth in his tent. Finally dawn comes, and Gideon in his Brooklyn Jewish accent cries out, "God, Oh God, all night long I've thought of nuttin' but You, nuttin' but You. I'm caught up in the raptures of love. God, I want to take You into my tent, wrap You up, and keep You all to myself. God, hey, God tell me that You love me." God answers "I love you, Gideon."
>
> "Yeh, tell me again, God."
>
> "I love you, Gideon."

Gideon scratches his head. "I don't understand. Why? Why do You love?"

And God scratches His head and answers, "I really don't know. Sometimes My Gideon, passion is unreasonable."[2]

The passion of God, which transcends human reason, elicits "the raptures of love," the passion of the beloved offering back herself or himself in grateful adoration. Alec Guinness wrote of his being on a London street soon after his conversion. He was filled with such exultant joy that he ran as fast as he could to enter a church, simply to be in the presence of the sacrament.[3]

Because we are loved by God, because God has embraced us with the grace of Christ, we respond instinctively with a joyous gratitude that expresses itself in praise—and we call this response worship.

THE JOY OF RESPONSE

Not only does worship happen in response to joy, joy happens as a result of worship; joy brings forth praise, and praise brings forth a new dimension in joy. My wife and I applauded Pavarotti out of joyous gratitude, but the applause itself swept us into more joy. Our exuberant ovation created its own happiness.

It felt good to praise Pavarotti because it *was* good. Not only does excellence deserve to be recognized and appreciated, human beings have a basic need to acknowledge it. God has created us for worship, for ascribing worth; to applaud glory is an essential part of our nature. We instinctively responded to the musical glory of Pavarotti because we have been made to praise the greater Glory behind it. The fountainhead of all other manifestations of glory in creation is the Holy One, the Light at the center, the Creator and Redeemer and Sustainer of our lives.

We have been created to live for the praise of this God. The New Testament tells us that God "destined us for adoption as his children through Jesus Christ, according to the good pleasure

of his will, to the praise of his glorious grace that he freely
bestowed on us in the Beloved. . . . so that we, who were the first
to set our hope on Christ, might live for the praise of his glory"
(Ephesians 1: 5-6,12). Our chief end, in the words of the Shorter
Catechism, is "to glorify God and to enjoy him forever."

The need for worship has been built within the nature of
our humanity. Even as cars need gasoline to run, and sailboats
need wind to sail, and hawks need thermals to soar, and fish
need water to swim—even so, we need worship to live. We
must worship; we *will* worship.

But not everyone worships God. This is because we have
the freedom to substitute any sort of false god for the true God.
G. K. Chesterton said that when we "cease to worship God, we
do not worship nothing, we worship anything."[4] And so in the
place of God, who alone deserves complete devotion, we erect
idols to receive our praise and adoration.

Imagine the crowd at a sporting event: a wide receiver
catches a pass and takes it over the goal line, or a guard sinks
a three-pointer from downtown, or a batter finds the meat of
a baseball and sends it into the next county—and the fans
jump to their feet and raise their arms in adoration. . . . In their
joy, they praise; in their praise, they have joy.

Imagine the audience at a rock concert: the lead singer
dances across the stage in a kind of frenzy, throwing parts of
his clothing to ecstatic supplicants, and the music is too loud
to hear but it doesn't matter because the fans are also too
loud, screaming in devotion to performers whose pictures
cover walls in their bedrooms. In their joy, they praise; in their
praise, they have joy.

We really can't help such behavior; to be human is to worship. What we can choose are the objects of our adoration. We
may worship God, or we may worship any number of false
gods. The gods of my cause, my understanding, my experience, my comfort, my nation, and my success are some of the
most tempting, as I have said. But others will work, too.
Money, power, sex—almost anything can take the place of
God. Thomas Aquinas said that no one can live without delight
and thus a man or woman deprived of spiritual joy will go
over to carnal pleasures.[5]

No false god, however, can supply the deepest delights of worship. We may aim adoration in a variety of directions, but the greatest joy comes to those who worship God. With the Light of Glory at the center, the lesser lights of glory shine brighter; with God the object of worship, life becomes what the Creator meant it to be. So Karl Barth described worship as "the most urgent, the most glorious action that can take place in human life."[6]

Evelyn Underhill wrote,

> Many a congregation when it assembles in church must look to the angels like a muddy puddly shore at low tide; littered with every kind of rubbish and odds and ends—a distressing sort of spectacle. And then the tide of worship comes in, and it's all gone: the dead sea urchins and jellyfish, the paper and the empty cans and the nameless bits of rubbish. The cleansing sea flows over the whole lot. So we are released from a narrow selfish outlook on the universe by a common act of worship.[7]

As worship re-orders our lives and washes away the debris—the sin that mars our humanity and sets in motion events that fall domino-like into brokenness and suffering—we recover our true selves; we inherit the joy for which we were created.

REVERENCE BEFORE THE WHOLLY OTHER

Yes, there is joy in worship, but this joy in no way cancels another primal emotion in the presence of holiness: an awe that improbably results from both terror and attraction. It's as though our joy in being saved by God's grace in Christ fills us with childlike abandon and we happily dance into the throne room of the universe. But once there, we suddenly become aware of our surroundings, conscious of our true situation, and we feel embarrassed and unworthy and even out of place. Worship has drawn us into an ever-deepening awareness of the mystery of God; our illusions of a manageable deity have been blown away.

God is so much more—more in every way—than we had imagined. Everything within us wants to back away from the danger. And yet, and yet. . . . We can't make ourselves move. We're terrified, to be sure, but there's more delight in the terror than we've ever before experienced. Not able to go forward toward the throne because of the fear, but also not able to move away because of the joy, we do the only thing we can do: we fall to our faces in awe. Only a God who is wholly other *and* wholly other-in-love could inspire such a response.

The trivial gods of our own making do not fill us with reverence. How could they? They remain under our control, subject to our desires, and thus they inspire a good deal of misdirected devotion from a culture in the thrall of scientific methodology, with its zealous dedication to control and explanation. The result, as I argued in chapter 1, has been a notable loss of awe; bullying empiricism has mugged mystery and left it lying with barely a pulse. To the extent that "mystery" means anything at all today, it likely brings to mind a detective novel or a thriller movie.

Longing for transcendence, however, cannot be repressed. Hunger for worship and the joy it brings remains buried deep within the human heart. And so these impulses occasionally get loose like wild horses breaking out of a corral: in addition to established religions and our own trivial gods, trendy spiritualities come and go, rising and falling with celebrity endorsements and cultic tragedies. These yearnings simply intimate we were made for something more, for Someone more, for an Other who exists wholly outside us and "above" us.

When this One seizes our attention through Jesus Christ, we may very well respond in joyous praise. But as this worship opens us to the presence of God, we find ourselves filled with fear. At least, we *ought* to be filled with fear. For if God is holy, our efforts to be like God are undone; if God is holy, our trivial gods are revealed as worth precisely nothing; if God is holy, the ground has been yanked out from under our feet and we are left hanging in the thin air of absolute vulnerability. "The fear of the Lord," we are told, "is the beginning of knowledge" (Proverbs 1:7).

No wonder, then, that when Isaiah entered the Temple to

worship and had a vision of the Lord sitting on the throne and heard the seraphim singing, "Holy, holy, holy is the LORD of hosts," the foundation of the thresholds shook and he cried out, "Woe is me! I am lost, for I am a man of unclean lips, and I live among a people of unclean lips; yet my eyes have seen the King, the LORD of hosts!" (Isaiah 6:1-5).

And yet this Lord has not allowed Isaiah or the rest of us to fall into the lostness we deserve, but has touched our unclean lips with a burning coal taken from the altar of holy love. Instinctive fear in the presence of the Wholly Other is then joined with an attraction for the Wholly Other-in-love, and we are filled with a respectful awe. When John of the Apocalypse was shown the reality toward which all things are moving, he too saw a throne room but was given a fuller vision than Isaiah's. He saw a triune God—the Father seated in regal majesty, surrounded by seven spirits representing the fullness of the Spirit, and near the throne stood the Son, the Lamb who had been slain. Falling before this three-in-one God were twenty-four elders and four living creatures and myriads of angels and countless worshipers—a vast choir embracing all creation—singing in reverent adoration, along with Isaiah's seraphim, "Holy, holy, holy."

Paul Jewett writes,

> This prostration in awe and boundless adoration on the part of the creation goes far beyond the commitment to some moral ideal. It reflects the awareness of what Otto has called the *mysterium tremendum*—the awesome strangeness, the fearsome otherness, the dreadful majesty of God; in short, his holiness, which makes him distinct from all others and comparable to no earthly being. . . . Even when this transcendent and mysterious God condescends to become one with us, he yet remains the One whose presence invokes reverence and awe. The more intimate the disciples became with Jesus, the less they understood him. . . . This sense of the divine as otherness is paramount in worship. Worship, indeed, is fellowship with God, the God who

has drawn near to us in Christ. But it is fellowship informed by reverence and awe.[8]

RECOVERING REVERENCE

Why, then, can you enter many a sanctuary on Sunday morning—formal or informal, liberal or evangelical—and find very little reverence? Respectable reserve may be there, but little, if any, flat-on-your-face awe; self-conscious dignity may hang in the air like incense after high mass, but nothing unsettling, nothing disorienting, nothing to strip away your certainties until your soul lies prostrate in naked embarrassment. You may find much good, such as vibrant fellowship or inspirational teaching or emotional music, but too much of it happens on the horizontal plane, with only a courteous nod toward the vertical. Chatty friendliness moves from the narthex into the sanctuary, intruding on preparation for worship. The purpose of the whole enterprise, it seems, is to guarantee that everyone feel comfortable and entertained.

Annie Dillard reflected on our pallid practice of worship:

> The higher Christian churches—where, if anywhere, I belong—come at God with an unwarranted air of professionalism, with authority and pomp, as though they knew what they were doing, as though people in themselves were an appropriate set of creatures to have dealings with God. I often think of the set pieces of liturgy as certain words which people have successfully addressed to God without their getting killed. In the high churches they saunter through the liturgy like Mohawks along a strand of scaffolding who have long since forgotten their danger. If God were to blast such a service to bits, the congregation would be, I believe, genuinely shocked.[9]

The trivialization of God inevitably leads to the trivialization of worship. The gods of our own creation—fitting neatly within the borders of our cause or understanding or experience, and serving well our comfort or nation or success—in no way transcend us, and for this reason they neither terrify nor attract us.

Reverence can be recovered only in repentance. To repent, in the language of the Bible, means to turn around, to turn away from one thing and toward another. The good news of Jesus Christ calls us to turn from false gods toward the holy God. And this demands a constant turning—we are never finished with the movement of repentance!—in which we consciously let go of the gods of our creation and re-orient ourselves toward the God of all creation.

This does not mean we should have doubts about whether God's grace continues to hold us. Anxiety has no place in our lives, for even the first baby steps of faith mean that we're part of the family, that God has begun a good work in us that will not fail, that Christ considers us his brother or sister and will for all eternity. But the self-centeredness at the core of our being is tenacious. Sin will continue to rear its ugly head until the day Christ returns and brings to fulfillment the salvation we now experience only in part. Thus we keep turning toward the Light at the center, toward the holy God of grace.

Repentance for people of faith usually begins with remembrance—recalling who we are and Whose we are. Recollection is not only a necessary daily discipline, but an important part of recovering reverence when God's people gather for worship. We must pause long enough to become aware of our actual circumstances: our joyous gratitude, we discover, has led us into the throne room of the universe, and now we are in the presence of the Holy One who utterly transcends us, who holds together all creation from the smallest molecule to the largest galaxy and all history from the first page to the last, who is burning in wrath against sin with the flame of purging love, who has claimed us in Jesus Christ and will keep us in the embrace of grace for all eternity—the God, in other words, who is far more than we thought we wanted but for that reason exactly what we really need to draw us out of ourselves and away from every trivial god.

In the presence of this God we may very well experience what Mole felt (if I may draw once more on the wisdom of *The Wind in the Willows*) when a great Awe fell upon him, "an awe that turned his muscles to water, bowed his head, and rooted his feet to the ground. It was no panic terror—indeed he felt wonderfully at peace and happy—but it was an awe that smote and held him, and without seeing, he knew it could only mean that some august Presence was very, very near."[10]

A chapel service during my year at Wheaton College had an unforgettable impact on me. The speaker was Dr. V. Raymond Edman, beloved past President of the College. His health had been precarious, and so it was a special moment when he stepped into the pulpit.

He wanted us to learn greater reverence before God. Worship is a serious matter, he told us, and to illustrate the point he recalled visiting Haile Selassie, then Emperor of Ethiopia. He described the preliminary briefings, the protocol he had to follow, and the way he bowed with respect as he entered the presence of the king. In the same way, he said, we must prepare ourselves to meet God.

At that moment Dr. Edman slumped onto the pulpit, fell to the floor . . . and entered the presence of the King of kings. He was dead, but for a few moments at least we had come to life. The dividing line between heaven and earth suddenly dissolved, and we were no longer restless college students with textbooks on our laps, worried about exams the next hour and dates the next weekend; we had joined angels and archangels around the throne.

When we gather for worship, whether we are immediately aware of it or not, we're about to meet the Wholly Other. Perhaps the most neglected opportunity in contemporary worship is the Prelude, the time in most services when the organ and chattering congregation compete with each other in crescendoing efforts to be heard. There are reasons for this, of course: today's architecture rarely inspires a sense of sacred space, and modern worshipers often commute long distances, making the first moments of gathering a sort of weekly reunion, a renewing of the bonds of fellowship. As understandable as this may be, though, we must nevertheless find ways of encouraging quiet reflection at the start of our services to enable us to remember that an august Presence is very, very near.

GOD-CENTERED WORSHIP

The repentance that recovers reverence begins with recollection and moves quickly to a singular focus on God. As we look up to the One seated on the throne, we lose sight of everything else; the Holy God commands and consumes our attention.

This may seem obvious. But sometimes, what passes for worship is more human-centered than God-centered. We want to make sure everyone "gets something" out of the experience, and for good reason: this tends to be the standard most of us use to judge whether a service was "meaningful" or not. Was *I* inspired? Were the sermon and music to *my* liking? Were *my* needs met? If not, well, there's always another church down the street to try next Sunday.

Much good results from the desire to be sensitive to the needs of the congregation, whether believers or seekers. Honorable motives may be at work and growing congregations the result. But what difference does it make if God is not at the center? What we really need when we show up for worship is for our attention to be turned toward the glory of God. Only in turning toward the Light can we do the dance, and only in this joyous but reverent dance before the Holy One will our deepest needs be met, for only then will we enter our full humanity as sons and daughters of God.

Søren Kierkegaard said we have gotten confused about who's doing what in worship: we think of worshipers as an audience; pastors as entertainers; and God as the prompter. In fact, worshipers are performers; pastors are prompters; and God is the audience. When we gather for worship, whether with a handful in a storefront chapel or with thousands in St. Peter's Square, we perform a drama with different parts—speaking and singing and praying and giving money and baptizing and eating bread and drinking wine—all for the delight of God. At the end of the show the only applause that matters comes from God.

It's worth staying with Kierkegaard's image a little longer. A drama takes place at a certain time and in a specific place. The actors and prompters and audience gather at eight o' clock, say, at the Old Globe Theater. And similarly, the worship of

God's people generally happens at a particular time and in a designated location. Not that we can't worship God anywhere at anytime; we can and must, because we have been called to offer our whole lives to God in the sacrifice of praise. But for this reason we set aside a specific place and time to witness to what we want to be true for all times and all places.

A husband and wife may love each other every day with steady commitment and mutual trust, but that does not mean they never set aside particular times and places for the special expression of that love. They have sexual intimacy, perhaps more or less according to certain patterns; they celebrate anniversaries and attend to other habits of devotion. Yes, even love has its rituals.

The word *ritual* has fallen on hard times. It usually follows a condemning adjective, such as "dead ritual" or "boring ritual" or "empty ritual." Forget ritual, we think. Leave that for stuffy traditionalists and strive for spontaneity! Such sentiments are nonsense. We need rituals; we can't live meaningful and productive lives without some sort of structure. Think through your day, and you will have to admit to engaging in a dozen routines before lunchtime. I typically start my day by getting out of bed and going downstairs to grind coffee beans and start the pot brewing. After taking a shower, brushing my teeth, and pouring a cup of coffee, I read my Bible and pray . . . every morning. These things are rituals, patterns that give my life order.

We dare not leave things we value most to vagaries of whim. So we join God's people at a certain time (most of us do this on Sunday, the day of resurrection) and in a specific place (this varies widely, from open fields to clapboard chapels to Gothic cathedrals). And when we get together, we practice our rituals of worship. Every service, whether a Pentecostal revival meeting on a sawdust trail or a Roman Catholic high mass with "smells and bells," has a structure, a pattern for praise. Even congregations that would never think of printing an Order of Worship because they consider themselves "free churches" nevertheless follow a predictable routine.

The choice, therefore, is not between structured or unstructured worship, but between thoughtful or unthoughtful structure. I'm no psychologist but I will venture a conviction: rituals of public worship deeply influence us, imprinting themselves on our subconscious minds and thus shaping the pattern of our personal spirituality. What we do corporately tends to set boundaries and create an ethos for what we do privately. A worship service that begins with exuberant hymns, for example, will teach that God should be approached with bold joy; a service that begins with confession of sin, on the other hand, will teach that we dare not approach God without honest self-examination and repentance from wrong-doing. Considerable attention should be given to the forms of praise we regularly employ, for they will significantly affect the dynamics of our relationship with God.

Ben Patterson tells a story of Abraham Joshua Heschel, the great Jewish rabbi, who was once confronted with a complaint from his congregation.

> Some of the members of the synagogue told him that
> the liturgy did not express what they felt. Would he
> please change it? Heschel wisely told them that it was
> not for the liturgy to express what they felt, it was for
> them to learn to feel what the liturgy expressed. As Jews
> they were to learn the drama and say it and "play" it
> over and over again until it captured their imagination
> and they assimilated it into the deepest places in their
> hearts. Then, and only then, would it be possible for
> them to live properly their own individual dramas.[11]

How should the community of worship structure its praise of God? It would be inappropriate for me to suggest one "proper" ritual. Cultural settings and personalities of congregations vary enormously—and this must surely please a Creator whose love of diversity manifests itself to even the most casual observer of nature. But this much can be said: all worship ought to be ordered *toward* God; services should be put together in a way that keeps our attention centered on God.

After Arturo Toscanini finished conducting a brilliant performance of Beethoven's Fifth Symphony, the audience rose to its feet and applauded, shouting its delight. But Toscanini waved his arms violently for it all to stop. He turned to the orchestra and shouted hoarsely, "You are nothing!" He pointed to himself and shouted, "I am nothing!" Then he shouted, "Beethoven is everything, everything, everything."[12]

Christian worship must say, "God is everything, every-thing, everything." What we do on Sunday mornings (or whenever we gather), the order of events and the manner in which we enact the drama, must always point to God, must reinforce again and again that God has taken the initiative and called us together, that God's grace is more important than our sin, that God's will is more important than our desires, and that God's glorification is more important than our edification.

This God-at-the-center worship happens only as we acknowledge another priority: God's Word is more important than our words. This Word alone—as it comes to us in Scrip-ture, sermon, and sacrament—has the power to turn us toward God.

CHAPTER NINE

Community
of the Word

To say that God's Word has priority over human words
may be true enough, but to modern ears it will likely
evoke nothing but a yawn of indifference. We're losing
interest in words of any kind. We have too many of them. The
information explosion has created verbal inflation, and consequently a devaluing of words. A popular country-western song
calls for "a little less talk and a lot more action," and though
the singer has something else in mind his plea might well rep-
resent the cry of a culture going down for the third time in an
ocean of words pouring in from telephones, televisions, radios,
faxes, and computers.

All this technology, we are told, is now being linked together
on an electronic superhighway that will speed us to . . . where?
Greater information, certainly. Greater networking, perhaps.
Greater wisdom? It's not likely. Words and the disparate facts
they communicate now come at us faster than we know how to
use them; we seem unable to tie them together into a meaningful whole. "Like the Sorcerer's Apprentice," Neil Postman
writes, "we are awash in information. And all the sorcerer has
left us is a broom. Information has become a form of garbage,

not only incapable of answering the most fundamental human questions but barely useful in providing coherent direction to the solution of even mundane problems."[1]

Ted Koppel, in an acceptance speech for the Broadcaster of the Year Award in 1986, observed, "What is largely missing in American life today is a sense of context, of saying or doing anything that is intended or even expected to live beyond the moment. . . . We have become so obsessed with facts that we have lost all touch with truth. . . . Consider this paradox: Almost everything that is publicly said these days is recorded. Almost nothing of what is said is worth remembering."[2]

We still use words, of course. Language forms the basis for much of our communication; we continue to have conversations, make and listen to speeches, read and write books, and depend upon the lingering power of words to create institutions like marriage (words of promise) and government (words of law). But currency in an inflationary economy stays in use, even though it declines in value; words may remain our primary unit of relational exchange, but their individual worth is declining.

The problem is that for all our words, we have no grammar of meaning, no way to tie together bits of information into sentences and paragraphs of truth. Relativism reigns. The quest for universal meaning has not only been abandoned, it has become an object of intellectual scorn. The dominant philosophy in many universities today is deconstructionism, the effort to de-construct literature and history and art (and all attempts to articulate truth) into atomistic bits of personal opinion and expressions of power. There is no language of truth, the deconstructionists tell us, only isolated words. And we have plenty of them.

THE WORD ABOVE ALL EARTHLY POWERS

We need no more words but a Word, an authoritative communication from outside our tangle of information that speaks the truth that can set us free, the truth that can save us by providing not just personal meaning but universal meaning, the meaning that ties all things together, things in heaven and things on earth, and therefore the meaning that can come only from One who is wholly other than us. We need what Martin Luther in his famous hymn called "that Word above all earthly powers" ("A Mighty Fortress Is Our God").

Many have despaired of ever hearing such a Word. After the travails of this century, God seems pretty distant. Woody Allen, in *Love and Death*, says, "If God would only speak to me—just once. If He would only cough. If I could just see a miracle. If I could see a burning bush or the seas part. Or my Uncle Sasha pick up the check."[3] We can understand these feelings. An unambiguous sign from God would surely be appreciated and would provide, we might think, just the solid foundation on which to build a spiritual life.

But if we join Woody Allen in waiting for God to speak in the extraordinary, we will likely miss the Word that has already been clearly addressed to us. When God speaks, as Elijah discovered, it's not usually in the wind or earthquake or fire, but in the realm of silence.[4] The Word does not blast away all doubt with unambiguous clarity and thus bully us into belief; instead, it takes the way of humility into this world, gently inviting us into a relationship of growing faith—a faith never without doubt as it moves steadily, if not always smoothly, toward deeper trust.

THE HUMILITY OF THE WORD

The Word which reveals everything we need to know about God and ourselves, and thus which reveals the grammar of meaning for all the words of our life, was spoken definitively in One who humbled himself from the height of glory to the shame and ignominy of a criminal's death. This Word was vindicated through resurrection from death, but the divine stamp-of-approval was not given for all the world to see; the resurrected Lord appeared visibly only to a few disciples and now "appears" invisibly to the rest of us who believe their testimony.

The Word continues to prefer the way of humility. But we must not be deceived: that which seems so weak has behind it the power of God. "God's foolishness is wiser than human wisdom, and God's weakness is stronger than human strength"

(1 Corinthians 1:25). Take every human-made sound uttered in this world, from the cry of a newborn baby to the deafening blast of a nuclear bomb, put them together in one cacophonous explosion of human self-expression—and it still doesn't even come close to the power in God's whisper, because the quietest Word of God has within it everything necessary for creation and redemption.

The first verses of the Bible tell us that God spoke the universe into being. God said, "Let there be light," and nothing sat up and became something, darkness blazed into luminescent brilliance. "God said . . . God said . . . God said . . ."—the phrase is repeated again and again in the creation story, as if to leave no doubt that God's Word alone brought all things into existence. You would never say to God, "a little less talk and a lot more action," for God's talk *is* the action. The psalmist proclaims that the entire universe was formed by the very breath of God's mouth.[5]

This Word constituted the people of Israel, promising and prodding them through history, and even when that history had seemed to fail them, when they were subjected to the humiliation of Babylonian captivity, it promised to do its saving business. Through the prophet Isaiah God said, It may seem as though you are defeated and that I am weaker than the gods of the invaders who have inflicted such suffering upon you, but you can count on what I'm telling you, for even as rain and snow water the earth, making it bring forth and sprout, even "so shall my word be that goes out from my mouth; it shall not return to me empty, but it shall accomplish that which I purpose, and succeed in the thing for which I sent it" (55:11).

This is the Word that became flesh and dwelt among us, the Word that not only announced the grace of God but did its work of salvation, the Word that entered sin-broken creation to bring about the re-creation of all things, the Word that defeated death and opened wide the gates to eternity, the Word that is not simply an item of information but a power "sharper than any two-edged sword" (Hebrews 4:12), the Word that could never come from the mouth of a trivial god but could only be the utterance of the Wholly Other One. And God continues to speak this Word to us. Though it still meets us in humble clothing, we should not be fooled by outward appearances; it has the power necessary to provide meaning for all other words.

Where do we hear this Word spoken? Do we hear it in our hearts? People will sometimes say things such as, "God led me to change churches," or "God told me to accept this job offer." Does God speak this directly to us? Does God's Word come to us through these inner voices? God certainly provides guidance for our daily lives, but how do we distinguish between the Spirit of God and the spirit of our own desires and hopes? Is it God leading me to a new church, or my own desire for novelty? Is it God leading me to a new job, or my own desire for advancement? The voices within compete for our attention. No wonder Scripture tells us to "test the spirits and see whether they are from God" (1 John 4:1).

Thankfully, God has graciously provided an external Word by which all inner words may be judged. This Word, which has been at work since the foundation of time to bring history to fulfillment in Jesus Christ, stands outside us, witnessing to what is authentically of God's Spirit within us. We can be confident that the inner promptings of the Holy Spirit will never contradict the external Word; God is one, and thus the Spirit works in concert with the Creator God who spoke into being the Word made flesh. All our feelings, therefore, and all our intuitions, sensings, inclinations, dreams, visions—all the inner voices— can be evaluated in the light of this external Word.

Again, the question: Where do we hear the Word of God spoken today? We can say that God speaks to us in a variety of means. But there are three primary ways in which the Word of God comes to us, each of them burdened with the weaknesses of human flesh in a continuing expression of divine humility. Today we hear the Word of God in Scripture, sermon, and sacrament.

THE WORD WRITTEN

The Bible is God's Word to us. We should not understand this in a mechanical sense, as though it were inscribed by angels and dropped from heaven. If the Book bears the authority of

Holy God, and thus can properly be called the *Holy* Bible, it does so because of a dynamic relationship between God and humanity. Only a wholly other God could deliver a Word that comes from outside us, a Word that transcends and judges and saves, and therefore a Word capable of delivering us from the trivial gods of our own making. And yet, because God is wholly other-in-love, this Word comes in a self-limiting humility that does not overwhelm but draws us into partnership in the events of revelation. God not only speaks *to* humanity but *through* humanity, using ordinary men and women bound to particularities of time and place as channels of communication.

God spoke through prophets who (consciously or not) were pointing toward the Word-made-flesh, and God spoke through apostles who were pointing back to that Word who had apprehended them in grace. And because God still speaks through them, their testimony is the Word of God in all its creative and saving power. Put in a slightly different way, the Living Word continues to humble himself, to clothe himself in human flesh, as he uses words written by his community to draw us into fellowship with God. The power that makes all this happen is God's Holy Spirit—the power that dwelt fully in Jesus Christ, the power that inspired the original prophetic and apostolic preaching and written record of it, and the power that now inspires our reading of these ancient words.

This holy commingling of human and divine speech is a miracle of grace. The Bible continues to provoke heated arguments over the precise nature of just what is human and what is divine in the historic origin and contemporary authority of the Scriptures. What should not be forgotten in this divisive debate is that the actual power of the Bible does not rest on any particular theology. In the words of P. T. Forsyth, "The authority in the Bible is more than the authority of the Bible; and it is the historic and present Christ as Savior."[6] The church did not first develop a theory of divine inspiration and then, on that basis, confer authority upon a canon of sixty-six writings; the church, rather, was confronted by an authority—apprehended by Christ!—in sixty-six writings that were eventually bound together in one book. The process was dynamic. The Bible, we could say, formed itself and asserted its own authority over the life of the community.

It still does. Charles Spurgeon once said, "The way you defend the Bible is the same way you defend a lion. You just let it loose." As the vehicle for the living Word of God, the Bible has within itself the power for creation and redemption.

During my years as a pastor, I often witnessed this power at work in people's lives. A woman once came to me, for example, and requested baptism. I asked her why she wanted to take this step, and she explained that she was a student at the University of California, majoring in Political Science. She had been a Marxist, but for one of her classes had to write a paper on Christianity. So, to be fair, she read the New Testament and it had changed her forever. She met Jesus Christ, who proved to be far more radical than Karl Marx.

This is why I always try to get skeptics to read the Book. When someone wants to debate the truth of Christianity by arguing about something like creation or the virgin birth, I acknowledge that these subjects may be interesting to discuss, but before we can proceed we really need to make sure we know what we're talking about. "Have you ever actually read the Bible?" I ask. Most often the person is relying on hearsay or a vague memory of Sunday school lessons. "Well then," I suggest, "why don't we read the Gospel of Matthew. Let's both try to be open: I will be open to its problems, and you be open to whatever truth it's trying to tell you." If the person agrees, I know he or she has started down the road toward quite an adventure. Again and again, I have witnessed the miracle of a life changed by interaction with the text.

The problem is getting people to read it. Bibles continue to be purchased, and they are set on coffee tables and occasionally sifted through for inspiration during times of stress. But biblical illiteracy is on the rise—even in the church. Bible studies have given way to support groups and classes on "practical" topics, such as parenting or coping with stress. Even pastors shy away from conferences offering serious biblical/theological reflection in favor of learning the latest techniques for church growth. And increasing demands on pastors—the call for administrators, fund raisers, counselors, and program developers—have left precious little time for studying the Bible.

Many factors undoubtedly have contributed to this neglect of Scripture. One, surely, is the advent of the information age and its consequent diminution of the significance of books. Another may be the growing dominance of the visual. We live in the video age, of course, and as Neil Postman has convincingly shown in *Amusing Ourselves to Death*, this has profoundly altered not only what we think but the *way* we think. We no longer think linearly (sentence by sentence, idea by idea); instead, we experience reality as a kind of impressionistic collage. So we are less inclined than ever to do the hard work of study. The Bible, when read, is rarely grappled with on its own terms in an effort to understand what it has to say; more often, it's approached as a kind of spiritual collage, as a suggestive resource to stimulate our own ideas or as a springboard for sharing personal experiences with one another.

How else can we account for the fact that about three-quarters of Americans say they have made a commitment to Jesus Christ, and yet only 13 percent believe the Ten Commandments are binding?[7] For all the warm feelings people have toward Christianity, apparently not many pay much attention to God's Word. The consequence is cafeteria-style religion, a do-your-own-thing spirituality that inevitably trivializes God to fit the contours of individual taste.

The most important step that could be taken toward removing trivial gods from the altar of devotion and renewing faith in the one true God, the Holy One, would be for the church to rediscover the Bible, to open itself anew to its creative and redeeming Word.

Gerhard Ebeling, in a lecture on Martin Luther delivered to all the faculties of the University of Zurich, asked, "Why did Luther's Reformation, in contrast to all prior attempts at reformation, become a reformation in deed and not just in words?" His provocative answer was, "Luther's Reformation became a reformation in deed and not just in words because Luther trusted only in the Word and not at all in deeds."[8]

Julius Hickerson was a promising young doctor who could have enjoyed a comfortable life in the United States, but he felt

God's call to serve as a missionary in Colombia, ministering to souls as well as bodies. His friends and associates thought he was crazy, and he himself must have wondered when, after two years, he could point to few visible results of his labor. It ended in tragedy as he was killed in a plane crash attempting to take supplies to a remote village.

But in the wreckage some natives found a well-marked Bible in their language, and they began to read it. They told others what they had read, and before long churches were started. The Southern Baptists, unaware of what had taken place, sent a missionary back into the area, and he discovered the place fully evangelized. When the missionary asked how it had happened, the Colombians showed him a Bible. On the inside of the cover was a name—Julius Hickerson.[9]

The written Word of God will not return empty.

THE WORD PROCLAIMED

The creative and redeeming Word of God continues to do its work through the proclamation of Scripture. This proclamation may happen in a variety of ways—personal witness to a neighbor, informal sharing in small groups, teaching in a classroom setting—but the term usually refers to the preaching of sermons, and for good reason: there is a fundamental difference between sharing personal experience or conveying information and the authoritative pronouncement "Thus saith the Lord." The preacher, called by God and set aside by the congregation for the task, listens with particular attentiveness to Scripture and then declares this Word to the community called together and indwelt by the Holy Spirit.

Biblical preaching does more than convey information about the Word; it is itself the Word, the power sharper than any two-edged sword, the power of the universe-creating, history-making, truth-telling, sin-annulling, death-defeating, life-giving, grace-granting, Kingdom-bringing Word. The Living Word continues to walk the road of humility as he speaks through the sermons of ordinary women and men.

This may seem an audacious thing for a preacher to write. But I'm simply passing on what the Christian community has understood to be happening in this strange activity that began with the preaching *of* Jesus—and then at Pentecost, in the power of the newly-descended Holy Spirit, became preaching *about* Jesus. "Every man who preaches the Word," declared Augustine, "is the voice of God"; "the preaching of the Word of God," Luther proclaimed, "*is* the Word of God"; according to Calvin, God "deigns to consecrate to himself the mouths and tongues of men in order that his voice may resound in them"; and "through the activity of preaching," Karl Barth contended, "God himself speaks."

Does this mean that every word in every sermon comes directly from the mouth of God? Of course not. We've all heard bad preaching; some of us have even committed it. Huck Finn commented that the farmer-preacher, Mr. Phelps, "never charged nothing for his preaching. And it was worth it, too." From a good many pulpits, it seems, one more often hears the voice of Mr. Phelps than the voice of God.

What Augustine, Luther, Calvin, and Barth were saying, however, was that in the event of preaching, in proclaiming the good news (gospel) of Jesus Christ, God's Word touches people with life-saving power. Despite weaknesses of the preacher (always considerable), and despite weaknesses of the hearers (also considerable), God's Word does its work. So Paul told the Thessalonians, "We also constantly give thanks to God for this, that when you received the word of God that you heard from us, you accepted it not as a human word but as what it really is, God's word, which is also at work in you believers" (1 Thessalonians 2:13). This is why Paul was not ashamed of the gospel, for it is God's power for salvation.[10]

As James Daane wrote,

> The Word itself creates its own hearing, as it once created its own world, by re-creating those through faith who once had no faith. Nothing more needs to be done; no homiletical gimmicks or artificial techniques are required to make the gospel effective. The gospel is mighty to work its way to those who have ears but do not hear. It breaks hearts of stone to create hearts of

flesh. "Is not my word like fire, says the Lord, and like a hammer which breaks the rock in pieces?" (Jer. 23:29).[11]

The preacher may be delivering a half-baked sermon, thrown together with as much doubt as faith, and the hearers may be distracted by strained efforts to quiet gassy stomachs or irritated from fighting with a spouse on the way to church or worried about a visit to the doctor, but when the gospel is preached, to use Bonhoeffer's image, Christ walks among his people. It's the miracle of Christmas all over again: Christ clothes himself in humanity, spurning the language of angels to speak with the tongues of mortals.

This does not happen easily; birth pangs are felt in polished pulpits as once they were in a crude manger. Preaching the Word of God involves pain—for both preacher and hearers. What flows through one person's mouth into the heart of another, after all, is the Word of the wholly other God, and that's bound to create a disturbance along the way.

On January 21, 1930, a historic radio broadcast was scheduled. King George was to address the opening session of the London Arms Conference, and for the first time the whole world was to be brought within the sound of the king's voice.

But this country almost missed it. A few minutes before the speech, a member of the control room staff at CBS tripped over the wire and broke it. The connection was severed.

Then Harold Vidian, chief control operator, grasped one of the broken wires in one hand and the other wire in his other hand, restoring the circuit. Two hundred fifty volts of electricity shot through his arms and coursed through his body, but he held on and the king's message was delivered to this country.[12]

That is a good image of what happens in the act of preaching. The one who would speak the Word of a wholly other God had better be prepared for a life-threatening jolt: the intersection between eternity and time, transcendence and immanence, heaven and earth, is a perilous place. May God deliver us from preachers insensible of the dangers. Those who are full of beans and confident in their gifts, who project an image of smooth certainty and easy familiarity with the Almighty, who demonstrate no agony of spirit or terror before the holy, had best start doing something more useful like pumping more honest gas. For the sort of gas they're pumping, despite the pulpit pounding and sanctimonious tone, is a god too trivial to take seriously. Preaching is an act of daring, declared Barth, and only the man who would rather not preach and cannot escape from it ought ever to attempt it.

"The office of preaching," Martin Luther said, "is an arduous task. . . . I have often said that, if I could come down with a good conscience, I would rather be stretched upon a wheel and carry stones than preach one sermon. For anyone who is in this office will always be plagued; and therefore I have often said that the damned devil and not a good man should be a preacher. But we're stuck with it now. . . . If I had known I would not have let myself be drawn into it with twenty-four horses."[13]

And more than a few hearers know what it feels like to be "stretched upon a wheel." Listening, too, is hard work, at least as difficult as carrying stones! It calls for more than concentration, which is hard enough; it demands attentiveness to another world—the world of the Holy—as the voices of this world speak loudly in our ears and the voices of our own self-centeredness whine like spoiled brats insisting on their own way. With this competition for our attention, how can we ever hear the voice of God?

I'm told that in some congregations in the Highlands of Scotland, the practice following worship services is not to tell the preacher "good sermon," but rather to say "I heard you well." But how can this happen? How can we hear well when so many other thoughts noisily wander through our minds, when we're reproaching ourselves for ugly thoughts we've had about a coworker or eyeing the shapely form of Mrs. Jones or organizing the preschool carpool or worrying about how to pay the bills with what's left in the checking account? When you think about it, it's a wonder anyone hears anything the preacher says on a Sunday morning!

I would totally despair of the situation, except for one fact: the Word of God does its business come what may. It's the Word of the holy God, and this means a Word that has more than enough power to prevail against all obstacles.

A few years ago, in a sermon on Romans 5:15-21, I spoke of how Christ fundamentally altered the human situation. While all had been marked by Adam's disobedience, now all have been re-marked by the grace of Christ's obedience. This means, I went on to say, that along with Paul we can regard no one from a human point of view. Christ has been crucified and raised even for those we don't much like. To illustrate, I gave a representative list of some people for whom Christ died: illegal migrants, the homeless, homosexuals, and so on. Nothing profound, in my view, surely nothing "prophetic."

The next day, though, I was chatting with an elder in the church. He said, "Don, about yesterday's sermon—I hated it." Coming from a man for whom I have deep affection, this hurt.

"I hated it," he repeated in case I missed it the first time. "The part about homosexuals. I can't stand them." His voice was getting loud, very loud. People in offices down the hall could hear us. "I CAN'T STAND THEM! AND I HATED YOUR SERMON!"

There was nothing but silence for a few seconds, and then he said in a soft voice, "But don't stop preaching the Word . . . because I need it."

A few weeks after that, following a worship service, I noticed him speaking with two members of the congregation, a father and his homosexual son who was battling AIDS. I wondered what would happen; I worried about what the elder might say. Then I saw him reach out and put his arms around his brothers in Christ as they bowed their heads in prayer. The Word was working, and a man was being changed.

The proclaimed Word of God will not return empty.

THE WORD DRAMATIZED

The Word of God encounters us in Scripture and sermon, and because we live not simply in minds but also in bodies, the Word of God also meets us in the sacraments. A sacrament is a visible sign of an invisible grace, a physical event conveying a spiritual reality.

Roman Catholics, Orthodox, and some Anglicans believe in seven sacraments—Baptism, Eucharist, Confirmation, Penance, Anointing the Sick, Matrimony, and Holy Orders.

Most Protestants accept only Baptism and Eucharist as sacraments, believing these were specifically commanded by Christ himself for the whole church. Though Protestants might see marriage, for example, as having a sacramental quality, they deny it is a true sacrament because it was given for all human beings (not simply the church) and it was not commanded for all believers (Christ himself was single). But the church, though disagreeing on the number of sacraments, has been united in understanding Baptism and Eucharist as central. My own Protestant convictions and the limitations of space will narrow my discussion to these two.

Dale Bruner has said, "The Sacraments are God's hugs . . . God physically approaching and touching us."[14] Baptism and Eucharist (also called the Lord's Supper and Communion) are mini-dramas of salvation using material props—water, bread, and wine (in some traditions, juice). By washing a new believer, and by eating and drinking together, Christians use their bodies to re-enact the story of God's gracious salvation in Christ. Through seeing, moving, touching, tasting, and smelling, God speaks again the creative and redeeming Word.

Calvin referred to the sacraments as "signs and seals" of God's grace. A sign points away from itself toward something else. Baptism witnesses to the cleansing from sin through Christ's death and resurrection. The Lord's Supper reminds us of Christ's body broken for us and his blood shed for us, and it directs our hope toward the banquet table of the Kingdom of God. The sacraments tell again the story of our new identity in Christ that we have heard in Scripture and sermon.

But they are more than signs; they are seals. Picture a scene from before the days of attorneys and notaries public. A king drips a puddle of hot wax onto a document, and then, as it cools, imprints it with his signet ring. The words on paper now have authenticity and carry authority. The Holy Spirit, similarly, uses the sacraments to confirm the truth of the gospel.

By faith alone we receive the full benefits of God's grace in Christ; the sacraments are not additional "works" we must perform to gain God's complete favor. But the Holy Spirit uses these expressions of faith to seal us with an assurance that we have been reconciled with God and adopted into the community of salvation. In this sense, these mini-dramas are a means of grace, a way in which the holy God transforms us into holy people.

Sometimes sacraments are called symbols. A symbol, as Paul Tillich taught, is more than a sign; it participates in the reality to which it points. The flag, for example, symbolizes our nation, and thus we do not want people to desecrate it. It carries a meaning greater than, say, a map of the fifty states (burn a map and no one will take offense). "Old Glory" is *part* of what it represents. Symbols play an important role in our lives, and for this reason, we treat them with respect. And none should be treated with greater respect than those given by God as doorways into the realm of the Holy. The wholly other God, who is wholly for us, humbly condescends to use for our good the mini-dramas of Baptism and Eucharist.

Water Baptism is the sacrament of initiation. Neither going forward at an altar call nor joining the membership rolls of a local congregation is the biblical sign of commencing Christian faith. We embark on the journey of discipleship through Baptism. It does not mark an arrival but a beginning.

Baptism has both an active and passive aspect: we submit to something done to us. By being immersed or sprinkled, we identify with Jesus and show our desire to follow him. Jesus was baptized by John at the beginning of his earthly ministry; by this ritual cleansing he identified fully with sinful humanity and revealed his complete submission to the will of God. Before his ascension to heaven, his parting instructions were "Go . . . and make disciples of all nations, baptizing them in the name of the Father and of the Son and of the Holy Spirit" (Matthew 28:19). So we baptize and are baptized in obedience to him.

The church has disagreed about the mode of baptism (must one be fully immersed or may one be sprinkled?) and about what to do with the children of believers (must they wait until they have faith or may they be baptized as infants on the basis of their parents' faith?). Important issues, certainly, but too often they have obscured the deeper meaning of the sacrament.

This ritual of washing signifies our cleansing through Christ, witnessing to our true identity. It thus proclaims the Word of God. Because this Word does not return empty but accomplishes God's purposes for salvation, Baptism *does* something—

effectively sealing our relationship with Christ, uniting us to him and his community. "Do you not know," Paul asked the Christians in Rome, "that all of us who have been baptized into Christ Jesus were baptized into his death? Therefore we have been buried with him by baptism into death, so that, just as Christ was raised from the dead by the glory of the Father, so we too might walk in newness of life" (Romans 6:3-4).

Warning: Baptism is dangerous. You would never know this from the way our culture has trivialized it into a sentimental rite for gushing over babies or marking an adolescent's rite of passage into the voting membership of a congregation. It is first of all "baptism into death," an identification with Christ's death as *my* death, a turning away from my old sinful self. Luther referred to baptism as "death by drowning."

Will Campbell tells the story of his baptism in the East Fork River in Amite County, Mississippi. In preparation for the event, his parents had ordered some clothes from the Sears & Roebuck catalogue to make sure that he would look good when he went under.

Will's brother, Joe, was a bit of a skeptic. Joe stood on the bank, watching the preacher baptize two or three other people before Will's turn. But as he watched, he got more and more worried for Will's safety. So he slid down the muddy bank and grabbed Will, saying, "Will, dear God, don't let them do this to you. A fellow could get killed doing this."

Will said, "It took me thirty years to recognize that was precisely the point."[15]

But though Baptism is "a watery grave," as Baptists once called it, it does not lead into a cul-de-sac of nothingness. We have been buried with Christ in Baptism, "so that, just as Christ was raised from the dead . . . we too might walk in newness of life." The sacrament puts more than water on us; it drenches us with the sign of Christ, and that means it seals us in holiness, marks us for all eternity as those who live in and for the Wholly Other One.

The Lord's Supper is the sacrament of continuing nourishment. Unlike Baptism, which happens to believers once at the start of discipleship's journey, we gather around the

Lord's Table again and again to be nourished along the way. Paul wrote to the Corinthians,

> For I received from the Lord what I also handed on to you, that the Lord Jesus on the night when he was betrayed took a loaf of bread, and when he had given thanks, he broke it and said, "This is my body that is for you. Do this in remembrance of me." In the same way he took the cup also, after supper, saying, "This cup is the new covenant in my blood. Do this, as often as you drink it, in remembrance of me." For as often as you eat this bread and drink the cup, you proclaim the Lord's death until he comes. (1 Corinthians 11:23-26)

Over this sacrament, too, the church has suffered disagreements leading to division. How should we understand the words, "This is my body"? Literally or figuratively? Roman Catholics maintain that the bread and wine actually become the body and blood of Christ; some Protestants say that Christ is indeed present in the elements, but in a more spiritual sense; other Protestants contend that Christ is present in the whole act of eating and drinking, rather like the host at his meal. But again the differences should not blind us to our essential unity: the church has always believed that this meal, when partaken in faith, makes possible intimate communion with Christ.

When we eat and drink, whether it be several times a year (as in some traditions) or every time the community gathers for worship (as in other traditions), we "proclaim the Lord's death until he comes." We *proclaim*. We engage in a mini-drama that preaches, that announces God's Word and therefore *does* something to us. In this act, the Living Word points us toward both the past and the future. At his table, Jesus Christ reminds us of his death for us, the offering up of his life in love for God and the world. And he reminds us that what began with his earthly ministry will one day be fulfilled when he comes again; then we shall eat and drink at the banquet table of the Kingdom of God. Time is relative, physicists say, and nowhere is this more true than when we sit at the Lord's table: past and future collapse into an eternal unity as the death and return of our Lord become present to us.

The God who is wholly other than us, whose love stands over against our self-centeredness, draws us into holiness through this meal. The table calls us out of solitary preoccupations into the fellowship of Jesus Christ. The Host of the Meal, who poured out his life for the world, now pours out his Holy Spirit, and the bond of love uniting Father and Son becomes the bond uniting us in a new community.

A friend of mine, Woody Garvin, spent his first years as a pastor working with Native Americans on the Hoopa Reservation in northern California. He tells of two young men who grew up in his congregation. Jimmy Brown was reared by his single mother, Marie. He had a small mental handicap, but had done well within his limitations; he was the night custodian at the Post Office, and had even become an elder in the little church.

Robbie Boyd was reared by his single father, George. Unlike Jimmy, he drifted away from the church, started drinking heavily, and fell in with a rough crowd. One night he and his friends went to the Post Office to harass Jimmy Brown. One thing led to another. They killed him.

Both families pulled out of the church, as might be expected. But some years later Marie Brown came back. And eventually, so did George Boyd. One Sunday George came late to the worship service, searched for somewhere to sit, and saw only one place left—next to Marie. So he took it.

That morning the congregation was celebrating the Lord's Supper. Woody wondered what would happen when the elements were passed, and what he saw was this: when George handed Marie the bread he said, "The love of Christ be with you," and she responded, "And with you." When he handed her the cup he said, "The peace of Christ be with you," and she responded, "And with you."

The dramatized Word of God will not return empty.

THE WORD AMONG US

The Word of God, in Scripture and sermon and sacraments, furthers its creative and redeeming enterprise among us. It speaks truth into the silence of a culture waiting to hear from God. Coming from the mouth of the Wholly Other One, it works against us, judging and putting to death our sin and the trivial gods we have made for ourselves. But because this is a judgment of grace, the Word also stands for us, saving and creating new life in fellowship with one another and with the holy God.

CHAPTER TEN

Community
of Love

W e are not the first generation that has attempted to
trivialize God into a more manageable deity. However, because we live in a century notable for its loss
of awe, its impatience with God's silence, and its rampant individualism, we have perhaps failed in this sin more than others.
We have fashioned gods to fit the contours of our desires and
then bowed before them with religious abandon: the god-of-
my-cause, god-of-my-understanding, god-of-my-experience,
god-of-my-comfort, god-of-my-nation, and god-of-my-success
have been our particular favorites.

Our malady suggests a good stiff dose of reverent agnosticism. We must recognize that on our own, we cannot scale spiritual heights to discover the true nature of God; sin has distorted our perspective, and thus we remain imprisoned in
ignorance. Our only hope is to listen attentively to the self-
revelation God has graciously given us in Jesus Christ. When
we do, we discover a God who is *fundamentally* different from
any god we might have created for ourselves—a holy God.

God's holiness means that God is separate, utterly distinct
from creation. But by keeping our attention focused on Jesus

Christ, we also affirm that God's otherness consists in a passionate desire not to remain separate but to draw us by grace into loving fellowship. The Wholly Other One is wholly other-in-love. Thus we may trust this holy God, confident we have been grasped by arms of grace and will be held for all eternity.

Turning toward the Center of creation, we become a new community. In a world lacking awe, we see a wholly other God who inspires reverent worship. In a world lamenting divine silence, we hear a wholly-for-us God who speaks a creative and redeeming Word. This Word meets us in what may seem the most unlikely of places—Scripture, sermon, and sacraments. We should not be deceived by this apparent weakness, for the Word bears within itself the power that brought the universe into being and thus is surely able to bring life-saving change.

What change needs to happen to us? Simply put, *God wants us to become holy.* In 1 Peter the church is exhorted "to be a holy priesthood" (2:5), grounded in the truth that it is "a holy nation" (2:9). In Ephesians, the opening paean to the God of grace declares that we have been chosen in Christ "before the foundation of the world to be holy and blameless before him in love" (1:4). The purpose of our election in Christ is that we should be holy before God. God's holiness establishes an answering holiness in the midst of creation. The holy Word creates a holy echo. The community—the church of Jesus Christ—is this holy response.

What does it mean for the church to be holy? Our understanding of God's holiness will guide us in this matter, for the people of God are holy in a derived sense, only as they in some way participate in the being of God. The church, accordingly, has tended to understand itself by one of the two main strands of tradition regarding holiness: the holiness of the church has most often been described in either religious or ethical ways.

THE CHURCH AS SET APART

The word *holy* originally referred to *"that which is marked off, withdrawn from ordinary use."*[1] In this early, *religious* meaning, holiness was "the great stranger in the human world."[2]

Some have understood the church's holiness in like manner; the church, they believe, is holy to the extent that it separates itself from the rest of the world. North American fundamentalism of the twentieth century offers the clearest example of this. "By the 1930s," George Marsden writes, "when it became painfully clear that reform from within could not prevent the spread of modernism in major northern denominations, more and more fundamentalists began to make separation from America's major denominations an article of faith. . . . Some fundamentalists were making separatism into a high principle."[3]

Not only did fundamentalists separate themselves from what they saw as doctrinally wayward denominations, they rigorously and rigidly marked themselves off from the surrounding culture, pointing to Paul's admonition, "What does a believer share with an unbeliever? . . . Therefore come out from them, and be separate from them, says the Lord, and touch nothing unclean" (2 Corinthians 6:16-17). Holiness was thus defined as separating oneself from the world, and this was usually defined in negative ways, what one did *not* do. The prohibitions were often trivial: a Christian did not smoke, drink, dance, play cards, or go to movies. Though fundamentalists would not have said avoidance of these activities constituted all there was to holiness, the prevailing ethos implicitly said as much. If nonChristians did these things, Christians did not. It took a good deal of creative proof-texting to make a biblical case against having a glass of wine or watching *It's a Wonderful Life,* but the issue had less to do with ethics than being separate.

The church in which I grew up was not especially strict, but I remember sitting in a side room while my third grade classmates learned to dance the hokey-pokey. A note from my parents excused me from this worldly behavior, and I had to run the record player with Elizabeth, who still spoke with a Norwegian accent, could beat up any boy in the school, and was part of a Pentecostal church. I don't recall whether I was more embarrassed at not being with my friends or afraid of being with Elizabeth, but I bravely carried my fundamentalist cross. I would never even have considered asking my parents if I could join my buddies on their Saturday afternoon visits to the

Bay Theater, that den of wickedness showing Disney movies. I was not bitter about any of this, for I was a Christian and Christians just didn't do certain things.

Perhaps I should use these childhood experiences as an excuse for my present weaknesses, especially my own failures as a parent; my inner child, after all, has no doubt been abused by these deprivations. But I bear no ill will toward my parents. They were simply using standards accepted by many Christians of that day, and moreover, they gave me a great gift: they helped me learn at an early age that being a Christian sets one apart from the rest of the world; bred in my bones was the conviction that disciples of Jesus Christ live differently than other people.

But though holiness, biblically defined, certainly refers to separateness, it knows nothing of separatism, of a withdrawing from the world. The ground of holiness is the holy God, the one whose separateness paradoxically manifests itself in the will not to be separate. A community that makes separatism an end in itself may very well find itself separate not only from the world but from the God who loves this world enough to send the Son to redeem it.

THE CHURCH AS MORALLY CLEAN

More widespread has been the church's understanding of its holiness as moral and ethical purity, as freedom from the stain of sin.

The difficulty with this approach, of course, is the obvious fact that the church is not free from sin. Though *by faith* we believe it wears the glorious raiment of Christ's righteousness, *by sight* we see it dressed in the torn and soiled rags of unrighteousness. Thus holiness must be seen as a matter of "more or less"—a quantity possessed in varying degrees.

Calvin believed the church is holy in the sense that it daily advances toward greater perfection: "It makes progress from day to day but has not yet reached its goal of holiness."[4] God graciously grants holiness in an objective, eschatological sense, but the church now experiences holiness only in part. "It is . . . true that the Church's spots and wrinkles have been wiped away, but this is a daily process until Christ by his coming completely removes whatever remains."[5]

John Macquarrie offers a more contemporary expression of this approach. Holiness, he tells us, "is very much a case of 'more or less,' and to many it will seem that the Church has often been less rather than more holy."[6] What does holiness mean? It means "being an agent of the incarnation, letting Christ be formed in the Church and in the world."[7] The results will be *ethical* in nature. The church will not always live according to proper moral standards, but one hopes that in the end achievements will overbalance failures.[8]

Understanding holiness as ethical behavior, however, trivializes it into moralism. Lose sight of the religious dimension—the sense of being separate unto God—and you will flatten the transcendent into a horizontal code of regulated behavior. Not only does this ignore a good deal of biblical material regarding the nature of holiness, it turns the Christian life into something safe and manageable: the rod of legalism deflects the lightning shock of the holy God.

If we quantitatively measure holiness against unholiness, we must ask: With what sort of scales is the judgment made? In the furnace of which—and whose—values has the weigh beam been cast? How many ethical deeds does it take to cancel out an unholy deed? The legalism implied in these questions has no place in the theology of either Calvin or Macquarrie, but the questions show the slippery slope we stand on when we define holiness in primarily ethical terms. At the bottom of the slope is the quagmire of moralism; we may grasp at branches of human wisdom, but they're too weakened by decay to save us from the mess.

HOLINESS AS GOD'S GIFT TO THE CHURCH

In what does the holiness of the church consist? Holiness can be reduced to neither separatism nor moralism, for it flows from the holiness of God. God is wholly *other*, to be sure, but in the paradoxical sense of being wholly *for*; God is separate precisely in the loving passion to overcome the separation. Two things can therefore be said about the church's holiness: the church is holy *because* God is holy, and the church is holy *as* God is holy.

God's holiness guarantees the church's holiness. What sets God apart from us is a love that will not let us stay apart, the love that has reconciled us in Jesus Christ, the love that liberates us through the Holy Spirit to be a community of faith and worship, the love that daily works in our lives through the creative and redeeming Word. The church exists not *despite* God's holy otherness, but *because* of it.

Holiness and grace can never be sundered, and therefore the church may never point to one part of its life and say, "This is holy and righteous" (as if it needed no grace), and to another part, "This is sinfully unholy" (and thus in need of grace). The church is the body of Jesus Christ—it comes into being through him and lives under his lordship—and because he personally embodies God's grace, it follows that the church subsists totally in grace and thus totally in the sphere of God's holiness. In itself, the church is sinful, but the church does not live in itself; it lives in the Lord.

Furthermore, the exact nature of the church's holiness cannot be known and measured by some sort of external ethical standard. God alone defines holiness. So to understand the church's holiness we must look to *the* event of divine holiness, to Jesus Christ. God's distinctive nature was revealed in Christ, and here we see a God of gracious love. Thus the church's holiness, too, can be understood neither as separatism nor as moralism, but only as love for the world.

As the church lives by faith in Jesus Christ and in the power of the Holy Spirit, it is holy. It is set apart from the world; as God grants the church holiness, it cannot fail to become different—perhaps not always visibly, but different in essence. This separateness, though, must not be confused with separatism, because its separation comes from existing in the Holy One "who, though he was in the form of God, did not regard equality with God as something to be exploited, but emptied himself, taking the form of a slave, being born in human likeness. And being found in human form, he humbled himself and became obedient to the point of death—even death on a cross" (Philippians 2:6-8). The church, as is true of its Lord, is wholly *other* as it is wholly *for*, separate from the world in its love for the world.

COMMUNITY OF LOVE

Self-centeredness in human hearts and individualism in contemporary culture create a loneliness that cries out for relief. James Baldwin captured this aching longing in a poignant description of a young man:

> The joint, as Fats Waller would have said, was jumping. . . . And during the last set, the saxophone player took off on a terrific solo. He was a kid from some insane place like Jersey City or Syracuse. But somewhere alone the line he had discovered he could say it with a saxophone. He stood there, wide-legged, humping the air, filling his narrow chest, shivering in the rags of his twenty-odd years, and screaming through the horn, "Do you love me?" "Do you love me?" "Do you love me?" And again, "Do you love me?" "Do you love me?" "Do you love me?" The same phrase unbearable, endlessly and variously repeated with all the force the kid had. . . . The question was terrible and real. The boy was blowing with his lungs and guts out of his own short past; and somewhere in the past in gutters and gang fights . . . in the acrid room, behind marijuana or the needles, under the smell in the precinct basement, he had received a blow from which he would never recover, and this no one wanted to believe. Do you love me? Do you love me? Do you love me? The men on the stand stayed with him cool and at a little distance, adding and questioning. . . . But each man knew that the boy was blowing for everyone of them.[9]

The church exists to answer that young man's question. By its proclamation of the gospel it points to the love of God in Jesus Christ and says, "Yes, you are loved, loved more than you can imagine, loved by a God who will never let you go." And because the church, too, lives by and in this love, because it draws its life from the Holy One, it becomes a company of prodigal lovers.

> Beloved, let us love one another, because love is from God; everyone who loves is born of God and knows God. Whoever does not love does not know God, for God is love. God's love was revealed among us in this way: God sent his only Son into the world so that we might live through him. In this is love, not that we loved God but that he loved us and sent his Son to be the atoning sacrifice for our sins. Beloved, since God loved us so much, we also ought to love one another. No one has ever seen God; if we love one another, God lives in us, and his love is perfected in us. . . . God is love, and those who abide in love abide in God, and God abides in them. (1 John 4:7-12,16)

Few words are forced to carry more meanings than *love*. We say, "I love chocolate ice cream," or "I love your new dress," or "I will love you for the rest of my life." The word gets dispatched to every front, forced to serve in every situation. But when we call the church a community of love, we have something very specific in mind. The New Testament writers picked up a rarely used Greek word—*agape*—and filled it with new meaning. Unlike *philos*, which refers to affection between friends, or *eros*, which refers to pleasurable attraction, *agape* means the sort of love we see in Jesus Christ: love that serves the needs of others.

Karl Barth described this love well: "*Agape* means self-giving: not the losing of oneself in the other, which would bring us back into the sphere of *eros*; but identification with his interests in utter independence of the question of his attractiveness, of what he has to offer, of the reciprocity of the relationship, or repayment in the form of similar self-giving." This love gives itself "in a pure venture, even at the risk of ingratitude."[10] "Self-giving has a most impressive sound. It smacks of heroism and sacrifice. But in reality it is nothing out of the ordinary. For to love and therefore to give ourselves is simply to affirm in practice that we do not belong to ourselves."[11] What does it mean to love one's neighbor? "To stand surety for him, to make ourselves responsible for him, to offer and give ourselves to him. . . . It consists in the fact that (whether he likes him and can earn his liking or not) the one interposes himself for the other, making himself his guarantor and desiring nothing but to be this."[12]

The church shows its holiness neither in separatism that withdraws from the world, nor in moralism that focuses on its own purity, but in self-giving love—a love that serves the needs of others, especially those ignored by a world that has no time for the unattractive, lonely, weak, and suffering. The Bride of Christ, with a profligacy blessed by the Groom, bestows her love even on the unlovable.

LOVE FOR ONE ANOTHER

We extend this love first to the community of Jesus Christ. "By this everyone will know that you are my disciples," Jesus said, "if you have love for one another" (John 13:35). As we turn back toward the Light at the center, we're able to see others in a new way, in the light of God's love, and we're able to hold hands; it's the way the dance must be done, holding each other's hands, because we're just learning the steps of faith and we're likely to trip and fall. We need each other for support.

In his novel *Walking Across Egypt*, Clyde Edgerton tells about Mattie Rigsbee, a woman in her late seventies who lives alone in simplicity and wisdom. At one part in the story, Mattie takes in a young scalawag, Wesley, who had escaped from a detention center. One Saturday night, she asks him if he has ever been to church. He says no; he has been by one, seen one on television, but never actually been in one. Edgerton then describes what went on in Mattie's mind:

> Mattie saw before her a dry, dying plant which needed water up through the roots—a pale boy with rotten teeth who needed the cool nourishing water of hymns sung to God, of kind people speaking to him, asking him how things were going, the cool water of clean people, clean children, old people being held by the arm

and helped up a flight of stairs, old people who looked with thanks up into the eyes of their helpers, of young and old people sitting together for one purpose: to worship their Maker, to worship Jesus, to do all that together and to care for each other and to read and sing and talk together about God and Jesus and the Bible. That would bring color to his cheeks, a robustness to his bearing. That would do it. He seemed smart enough. And, since he hadn't been to church, then he was lost; this could be his first stop on the road to salvation.[13]

The community of Jesus Christ is an extended family, and like most families, we don't always love as well or wisely as we ought; sometimes we're too preoccupied with our own problems, and sometimes we're just weary and even irritated with each other. But when we see the waters wash over a new believer, we're reminded that Baptism has given us a new name—Christian—and conferred on us an identity we can't deny, and when we sit at table for Supper, eating and drinking together in the name of our Elder Brother, we come to our senses and once more take up the towel to wash the dirty feet of our brothers and sisters.

I think of Frank. He's a hard-driving corporate attorney, a can-do personality who goes at everything with a "take no prisoners" dedication. A few years ago he felt the Lord calling him to give himself in a deeper way to someone in need, and so he picked Steve, a young man dying of A.L.S. (Lou Gehrig's disease), and cared for him and helped him until the paralysis squeezed the last breath out of Steve.

After Steve's death, Frank moved on to Howard, who had been diagnosed with cancer. He stuck with Howard, too, holding his hand until the day it grew limp and cold. And then, with Howard dispatched to the Lord's eternal embrace, Frank turned his energies toward Bill, a well-known doctor in his late fifties who had just been diagnosed with Alzheimer's disease. "This is going to be tough," he told me, "but I've signed on for the long haul." And he has stayed with Bill and his family through the most horrific suffering imaginable. He even flew with Bill to Arizona to watch the San Diego Padres in spring training. When they returned, he said, "Don, we sure had some *interesting* experiences, but it was great! I took my son with us, because I wanted to show him that this is just what disciples of Jesus do, that we're to love one another. Don, as my Pop used to say, 'We're rich. And someday we're going to have money.'"

When Bill dies, Frank will find someone else in whom to invest his life. It's what the community does for one another.

LOVE FOR THE WORLD

The community also extends its love to those who have not yet taken their place at the family table. The church, after all, can hardly turn its back on the ones for whom its Lord died. Holiness manifests itself in God-like love for the world, in a passionate commitment to grasp the hands of those not yet in the circle, and by ministering to their deepest needs, draw them into the dance.

Richard Selzer, a surgeon with an extraordinary gift of writing, describes a memorable scene:

I stand by the bed where a young woman lies, her face postoperative, her mouth twisted in palsy, clownish. A tiny twig of the facial nerve, the one to the muscles of her mouth, has been severed. She will be thus from now on. The surgeon had followed with religious fervor the curve of her flesh; I promise you that. Nevertheless, to remove the tumor in her cheek, I had to cut the little nerve.

Her young husband is in the room. He stands on the opposite side of the bed, and together they seem to dwell in the evening lamplight, isolated from me, private. Who are they, I ask myself, he and this wry-mouth I have made, who gaze at and touch each other so generously, greedily? The young woman speaks.

"Will my mouth always be like this?" she asks.

"Yes," I say, "it will. It is because the nerve was cut."

She nods and is silent. But the young man smiles.

"I like it," he says. "It is kind of cute."

All at once I *know* who he is. I understand, and I
lower my gaze. One is not bold in an encounter with a
god. Unmindful, he bends to kiss her crooked mouth,
and I am so close I can see how he twists his own lips
to accommodate to hers, to show her that their kiss still
works.[14]

The church, in the passion of true holiness, kisses the
world, twisting its lips to accommodate a crooked, needy
mouth.

So William Booth gave himself to the "Vermin-eaten saints
with moldy breath,/ Unwashed—legions with the ways of
death" [15] on the streets of London. And Damien volunteered to
live among the lepers of Molokai (with the certainty of becom-
ing a leper himself). And Albert Schweitzer—musician,
scholar, medical doctor—turned his back on the comforts of
Europe to sail for Africa. And Sister Immanuel, at the age of
sixty-four, asked her superiors for the privilege of working
with the garbage pickers in Cairo, Egypt, to educate their children, tell them about Jesus, and help them sort garbage. And
Mother Teresa established a home in Calcutta so the most
wretched there could die within sight of loving eyes.

These saints—these holy ones—are well known. But
Christ's people usually do their loving in obscurity. The congregation where I served as pastor, to mention but one local
community, was filled with people deeply committed to telling
others about the love of God and to demonstrating that love
by helping people in their darkest hours of need.

Examples come to mind faster than I can write. Catherine
started an outreach to singles, and out of it grew a Divorce
Recovery Workshop, which ministered so powerfully to the
bruised in spirit that she and her team did it again, and then
again, and they're still going strong, helping piece together broken lives.

Virginia, whose comfort was disturbed by one of my sermons, was not able to sleep for several nights, worrying about
the hungry in our community. Why doesn't somebody help
them? she wondered. Then she seemed to hear the Lord ask,
"Why don't *you* help them?" She wasn't sure what she could do.

She knew she couldn't solve the problem of world hunger, and she knew she didn't have answers for the political and social issues surrounding illegal immigration, but she also knew there were migrants not far from her house who didn't have enough to eat. She could at least feed a few people. So she started making sandwiches to distribute one day a week. Eventually friends began to help; her kitchen became a busy place of slinging tuna fish and spreading love. Word passed quickly through the camps, and now migrants know where to get a lunch.

Olive started warning us about a frightening new disease called AIDS when most of us knew very little about it. She wouldn't let us keep our heads in the sand; she insisted we hold a conference on the subject, both for education and for developing a strategy to help those who become infected. We did that, and out of it emerged a ministry that created first a home for adults dying with AIDS and then a home for infants whose lives would be cut tragically short by the disease.

Aubrey makes money by building doll houses but makes a living by caring for the poor. He began his ministry by filling a car with day-old bread and taking it across the border to Tijuana. It was a classic case of "one thing leads to another": soon he was filling a van, and before long—this is the honest truth!—he was filling jumbo jets (747s and DC10s) with food for Africa and Eastern Europe. With a childlike trust in God, he has a way of cutting through bureaucratic red tape and corruption that must surely make the angels giggle. A couple of years ago he challenged the congregation to help him feed the hungry in Los Angeles and San Diego (Aubrey never thinks small); he said he had a hunch that growers and distributors in the San Joaquin Valley would be willing to help us, and he convinced the elders to lease a diesel truck and trailer. I'll never forget when it first rolled into our parking lot filled with 40,000 pounds of bananas. Soon Aubrey found vegetables and other good things, the congregation bought a diesel tractor with two trailer rigs, and now they move at least 100,000 pounds of food a week.

I could go on to mention homeless shelters, mobile medical teams for migrants in the hills, and grief support groups. And the story of Solana Beach Presbyterian Church is repeated many times over in congregations all around the world, because the community of Christ, being a holy community, gives itself in love.

It's not that the Christians have a naive dream of solving all the problems of the world; in fact, they have a blessed freedom from calculating success and failure. Someone once asked Mother Teresa, "How do you stand it? Here you are in Calcutta. You probably don't touch more than one percent of the suffering and dying in the city." Mother Teresa replied in words that are now famous, "I was not called to be successful; I was only called to be faithful."

The community of Christ loves because God has drawn it into the realm of holiness, because it has its center of gravity in Jesus Christ, the One who told of a coming judgment in which he "will say to those at his right hand, 'Come, you that are blessed by my Father, inherit the kingdom prepared for you from the foundation of the world; for I was hungry and you gave me food, I was thirsty and you gave me something to drink, I was a stranger and you welcomed me, I was naked and you gave me clothing, I was sick and you took care of me, I was in prison and you visited me.' And when the righteous will ask when they did all these things, the king will answer, 'Truly I tell you, just as you did it to one of the least of these who are members of my family, you did it to me'" (Matthew 25:34-40).

THE DISRUPTIVE POWER OF LOVE

Trivial gods may prove useful in many ways; manageable deities can serve our desires, providing religious inspiration without any unsettling disorientation. But in the end, though they often give us what we want, they can't deliver what we need.

Only the Holy One transcends us enough to save us from the self-centeredness that destroys human community and leads to death. This salvation begins with nothing less than the undoing of our lives. Meeting the Wholly Other One will cause the greatest disruption we can experience, for we will be forced to let go of our cherished gods, to let go even of ourselves.

But when we discover this God is wholly other-in-love, we

can do no other than capitulate in response to such love. We know we must turn our lives around in faith. That turning toward the Center enables us to join hands with a new community—a community of worship, a community of the Word, and a community of love.

Walter Ulbricht, the former leader of East Germany, once had a conversation with Karl Barth about the new society that was being built in his communist country. Ulbricht boasted that the Party would be teaching the Ten Commandments in the schools and that the Decalogue would provide the moral foundation for their new society. Barth listened politely and then said, "I have only one question, Mr. Minister: will you also be teaching the First Commandment?"

I am the LORD *your God; you shall have no other gods before me*—will this commandment be first in our lives?

Notes

One—The Trivialization of God

1. Annie Dillard, *Teaching a Stone to Talk* (New York: Harper & Row, 1982), pp. 40-41.
2. Albert Einstein, as quoted in *Bits and Pieces*, August 1989, p. 15.
3. As quoted by John Gardner, *On Leadership* (New York: The Free Press, 1990), p. 11.
4. Stephen Jay Gould, as quoted in "The Meaning of Life," *Life*, December 1988, p. 84.
5. See Paul K. Jewett, *God, Creation, and Revelation—A Neo-Evangelical Theology* (Grand Rapids: Eerdmans, 1991), pp. 200-201.
6. Frederick Buechner, *Son of Laughter* (San Francisco: HarperCollins, 1993), pp. 131-132.
7. Charles Williams, *The Place of the Lion* (Grand Rapids: Eerdmans, 1974), pp. 74-75.
8. Elie Wiesel, *Night* (New York: Bantam, 1960), pp. 72-73.
9. Arthur Miller, *Timebends* (New York: Harper & Row, 1987), p. 482.
10. As quoted by William E. Hulme, *Managing Stress in*

Ministry (San Francisco: Harper & Row, 1985), p. 108.

11. Jewett, *God, Creation, and Revelation*, p. 174.
12. *Leadership Journal*, Fall 1990, p. 129.
13. Neil Postman, *Technopoly* (New York: Alfred A. Knopf, 1992), pp. 69-70.
14. Robert Bellah, et al., *Habits of the Heart—Individualism and Commitment in American Life* (Berkeley: University of California, 1985), pp. 232-233.
15. Bellah, *Habits of the Heart*, pp. 232-233.
16. Bellah, *Habits of the Heart*, pp. 232-233.
17. Harold Bloom, *The American Religion—The Emergence of the Post-Christian Nation* (New York: Simon & Schuster, 1992), p. 15.
18. Kenneth Grahame, *The Wind in the Willows* (London: Methuen Children's Books Ltd, Magnet Reprint Edition, 1978), pp. 134-136.

Two—A Pantheon of Deities

1. See Psalm 24:1; Isaiah 58:6-7.
2. Gustavo Gutierrez, *A Theology of Liberation*, Caridad Inda and John Eagleson, trans. and ed. (London: SCM Press Ltd, 1974), pp. 155-156.
3. Lesslie Newbigin, *The Gospel in a Pluralistic Society* (Grand Rapids: Eerdmans, 1989), p. 150.
4. Janet Martin Soskice, "Can a Feminist Call God 'Father'?" *Speaking the Christian God—The Holy Trinity and the Challenge of Feminism*, Alvin F. Kimmel, Jr., ed. (Grand Rapids: Eerdmans, 1992), p. 86.
5. Rosemary Radford Ruether, *Women-Church: Theology and Practice* (San Francisco: Harper & Row, 1985), p. 104, as quoted by Elizabeth Achtemeier, "Exchanging God for 'No Gods'," *Speaking the Christian God*, p. 12.
6. Sallie McFague, *Models of God—Theology For an Ecological, Nuclear Age* (Philadelphia: Fortress Press, 1987), pp. xi, 14ff.
7. As quoted by John P. Diggins, *The Lost Soul of American Politics* (New York: Basic, 1984), p. vii.
8. George M. Marsden, *Reforming Fundamentalism* (Grand Rapids: Eerdmans, 1987), p. 148.

9. Marsden, *Reforming Fundamentalism*, p. 149.
10. Diogenes Allen, *Temptation* (Cambridge: Cowley, 1986), pp. 62-63.
11. Ben Patterson, *The Grand Essentials* (Waco: Word, 1987), p. 146.
12. Eberhard Busch, *Karl Barth*, trans. John Bowden (Philadelphia: Fortress, 1976), p. 489.
13. Dennis and Rita Bennett, *The Holy Spirit and You* (South Plainfield: Bridge, 1971), pp. 64-65.
14. The exegetical case for speaking in tongues as the necessary sign of Spirit baptism usually rests on *The Acts of the Apostles*. Speaking in tongues accompanied the descent of the Holy Spirit three times in Luke's narrative of the early church (Acts 2, 10, 19). But most commentators believe these refer to historic instances showing how the gift of the Spirit was for the whole church and how the Spirit was helping the church fulfill the Lord's command to be his witnesses "in Jerusalem, in all Judea and Samaria, and to the ends of the earth" (Acts 1:8). The question may well be asked, If this gift is normative for the whole church, why doesn't the New Testament discuss it in a prescriptive as well as descriptive manner? The one time it is dealt with prescriptively is in 1 Corinthians 14, where Paul urges caution in its use.
15. John Killinger, "When We Stop Being Free," *Pulpit Digest*, July/August 1992, pp. 12-13.

Three—In the Temple of Idols
1. Os Guinness, "America's Last Men and Their Magnificent Talking Cure," *No God But God—Breaking With the Idols of Our Age*, ed. Os Guinness and John Seel (Chicago: Moody, 1992), pp. 111-112.
2. Guinness, *No God But God*, p. 116.
3. As quoted by Thomas Long, "God Be Merciful to Me, a Miscalculator," *Theology Today*, July 1993, p. 166.
4. Philip Rieff, *The Triumph of the Therapeutic—Uses of Faith after Freud* (Chicago: University of Chicago, 1966, 1987).
5. Robert Wuthnow, "Small Groups Forge New Notions of Community and the Sacred," *Christian Century*,

December 8, 1993, pp. 1239-1240.

6. Kim Hall, interviewed in *The Door,* September-October 1992, quoted in "Reflections," *Christianity Today,* August 16, 1993, p. 33.

7. C. S. Lewis, *The Problem of Pain* (New York: Macmillan, 1962), p. 41.

8. Russell Baker, *Good Times* (New York: Plume, 1990), p. 231.

9. As quoted by Tom Sine, "God's Will—And a Little Creativity," *Christianity Today,* February 17, 1989, p. 24.

10. *Preaching,* January/February 1987, p. 53.

11. As quoted by Ernest T. Campbell, *Locked in a Room with Open Doors* (Waco, TX: Word, 1974), p. 23.

12. Cited by James Bell, "The Baby Boomer Cultural Ethos," *Bridge Over Troubled Water* (Wheaton, IL: Victor Books/SP Publications, 1993), page 73.

13. Gloria Copeland, *God's Will Is Prosperity* (Fort Worth: KCP Publications, 1978).

14. Russell Chandler, *Racing Toward 2001* (Grand Rapids: Zondervan, 1992), p. 308.

15. Dan Wakefield, *Returning—A Spiritual Journey* (New York: Doubleday, 1988), pp. 198-199.

16. J. B. Phillips, *The Price of Success* (Wheaton, IL: Harold Shaw, 1984).

17. As quoted by Daniel J. Boorstin, *The Americans—The Colonial Experience* (New York: Vintage Books, 1958), p. 3.

18. Boorstin, *The Americans,* p. 5.

19. Roger Finke and Rodney Stark, *The Churching of America, 1776–1990* (Rutgers University Press, 1992), as quoted in *Leadership,* Summer 1993, p. 76.

20. Chandler, *Racing Toward 2001,* p. 15.

21. James Patterson and Peter Kim, *The Day America Told the Truth: What People Really Believe About Everything That Really Matters* (New York: Prentice Hall, 1991).

22. Donald G. Bloesch, "No Other Gospel," *Presbyterian Communiqué,* January /February 1988, p. 8.

23. P. J. O'Rourke, *Parliament of Whores* (New York: Atlantic Monthly, 1991), p. 121.

Four—In Praise of Agnosticism

1. Paul Davies, *The Mind of God* (New York: Simon & Schuster, 1992), as quoted in *The Living Pulpit*, April/June 1992, p. 7.
2. Donald Bloesch, *A Theology of Word and Spirit—Authority and Method in Theology* (Downers Grove, IL: InterVarsity, 1992), p. 182.
3. Paul K. Jewett, *God, Creation, & Revelation—A Neo-Evangelical Theology* (Grand Rapids: Eerdmans, 1991), p. 86.
4. Dietrich Bonhoeffer, *Letters and Papers from Prison*, Reginald Fuller, et al., trans. (London: SCM Press, 1971), p. 300.
5. As quoted by H. Richard Niebuhr, *Radical Monotheism & Western Culture* (New York: Harper, 1943), p. 123.
6. As quoted by Ben Patterson, *Waiting—Finding Hope When God Seems Silent* (Downers Grove, IL: InterVarsity, 1989), p. 53.
7. James Davison Hunter, *Culture Wars—The Struggle to Define America* (New York: BasicBooks, 1991), p. 50.
8. See Robert Wuthnow, *The Struggle for America's Soul—Evangelicals, Liberals, and Secularism* (Grand Rapids: Eerdmans, 1989).
9. Richard J. Mouw, *Uncommon Decency—Christian Civility in an Uncivil World* (Downers Grove, IL: InterVarsity, 1992).
10. Freeman Patterson, *Photography and the Art of Seeing* (Philadelphia: Chilton Books, 1965), p. 9.

Five—The Self-Revelation of God

1. John W. Yates II, "Christ's Birth and Your Birth," 1990, *Preaching Today*, tape no. 87.
2. Ludwig Feuerbach, *The Essence of Christianity*, G. Eliot, trans., as quoted by Ferguson, et al., *New Dictionary of Theology* (Downers Grove, IL: InterVarsity, 1988), p. 259.
3. John Milton, from "On the Morning of Christ's Nativity," in *The Norton Anthology of Poetry*, ed. Alexander W. Allison, et al. (New York: Norton, 1975), p. 310.
4. Heinz Zahrnt, *The Question of God—Protestant Theology in the Twentieth Century* (London: Collins, 1969), p. 15.
5. Friedrich Schleiermacher, *The Christian Faith*, H. R.

Mackintosh and J. R. Stewart, ed., D. M. Baillie, et al.,
trans. (Edinburgh: T. & T. Clark, 1928), p. 264.

6. T. F. Torrance, *Karl Barth—An Introduction to His Early Theology, 1910–1931* (London: SCM Press, 1962), p. 31.

7. Karl Barth, *The Word of God and the Word of Man*, Douglas Horton, trans. (London: Hodder & Stoughton, 1928), p. 196.

8. Karl Barth, *The Epistle to the Romans*, Edwin C. Hoskyns, trans. (London: Oxford, 1933).

9. Barth, *Romans*, p. 29.

10. "The Theological Declaration of Barmen," as quoted in *The Book of Confessions—Presbyterian Church (USA)*.

11. As told by Maxie Dunnam, *Jesus's Claims—Our Promises*, cited in *Leadership*, Winter 1988, p. 37.

12. John Macquarrie, *Principles of Christian Theology* (London: SCM Press, 1966), p. 284.

13. Macquarrie, *Principles of Christian Theology*, p. 276.

14. C. S. Lewis, *The Horse and His Boy* (Middlesex: Puffin, 1954), p. 167-169.

15. Paul K. Jewett, *God, Creation, & Revelation—A Neo-Evangelical Theology* (Grand Rapids: Eerdmans, 1991), p. 176.

16. Helmut Thielicke, *The Evangelical Faith—Volume 2* (Grand Rapids: Eerdmans, 1977), p. 268.

17. Freeman Patterson, *Photography and the Art of Seeing* (Philadelphia: Chilton Books, 1965), p. 9.

18. John P. Meier, *A Marginal Jew—Rethinking the Historical Jesus* (New York: Doubleday, 1991).

19. John Dominic Crossan, *Jesus: A Revolutionary Biography* (San Francisco: Harper, 1994).

Six—Consuming Fire

1. Quotations are from Luke 1:35, 4:34; John 6:68.

2. Frederick Dale Bruner, *The Christbook—A Historical/Theological Commentary* (Waco, TX: Word, 1987), pp. 241-242.

3. Walter Eichrodt, *Theology of the Old Testament*, vol. I, trans. J. A. Baker (London: SCM Press, 1961), p. 270.

4. Gerhard von Rad, *Old Testament Theology*, vol. I, D. M. G. Stalker, trans. (Edinburgh and London: Oliver & Boyd,

1962), p. 205.

5. O. Procksch, *"hagios,"* in *Theological Dictionary of the New Testament*, vol. I, Gerhard Kittel, ed., Geoffrey W. Bromiley, trans. (Grand Rapids: Eerdmans, 1964), pp. 89-94. My analysis of the biblical meaning of "holiness" is very much indebted to this excellent linguistic and theological study.

6. See Exodus 3:5; Nehemiah 11:1,18; Psalm 28:2; and Isaiah 11:9; 48:2; 56:7; 64:10.

7. See Leviticus 2:3,10; 7:1; 16:4; 16:16-17; 23:4; and 27:30.

8. The succeeding citations are from Hosea 6:10; 9:14; 14:1; 11:1-4; and 6:1.

9. Eichrodt, *Old Testament Theology*, vol. I, p. 281.

10. Procksch, *"hagios,"* p. 93.

11. See Isaiah 41:14, 43:13-15, 47:4, 48:17, 49:7, 59:20.

12. Procksch, *hagios*, p. 94.

13. Rudolf Otto, *The Idea of the Holy—An Inquiry into the Non-Rational Factor in the Idea of the Divine and Its Relation to the Rational*, John W. Harvey, trans. (London: Oxford, 1923), pp. 6-7, 10.

14. Otto, *The Idea of the Holy*, pp. 12 ff.

15. Otto, *The Idea of the Holy*, p. 31.

16. L. M. Montgomery, *Emily of New Moon* (New York: F. A. Stokes, 1923), p. 7.

17. Abraham J. Heschel, *The Prophets* (New York: Harper & Row, 1962), p. 227.

18. Paul Tillich, *Systematic Theology*, vol. I (Chicago: Univ. of Chicago, 1951), p. 217.

19. Heinrich Heppe, *Reformed Dogmatics*, rev. and ed. Ernst Bizer, G. T. Thompson, trans. (London: George Allen & Unwin Ltd, 1950), p. 92.

20. See, e. g., Albert C. Knudson, *The Doctrine of God* (New York; Abingdon Press, 1930), pp. 335-336 (Methodist); Edward Arthur Litton, *Introduction to Dogmatic Theology*, ed. Philip E. Hughes (London: James Clarke, 1960), p. 71 (Anglican); Ernest Swing Williams, *Systematic Theology*, vol. I (Springfield: Gospel Publishing House, 1953), p. 187 (Pentecostal).

21. William Newton Clarke, *The Christian Doctrine of God*

(Edinburgh: T. & T. Clark, 1909).

22. See Isaiah 6:1-5.

23. C. S. Lewis, *The Lion, the Witch, and the Wardrobe* (London: Puffin, 1950), p. 75.

Seven—Conversion into Community

1. John Calvin, *Institutes of the Christian Religion*, John T. McNeill, ed., Ford Lewis Battles, trans. (Philadelphia: The Westminster Press, 1960), pp. 37-38.

2. As quoted by Tom Long, "Editorial," *Theology Today*, July 1993, p. 167.

3. As quoted by Cornelius Plantiga, Jr., "Not the Way It's S'pposed to Be: A Breviary of Sin," *Theology Today*, July 1993, pp. 179-180.

4. Donald Baillie, *God Was in Christ* (New York: Charles Scribner's & Sons, 1948), p. 205.

5. Annie Dillard, *The Living*, as quoted by Dave Goetz, in *Leadership*, Winter 1993, p. 48.

6. C. S. Lewis, *The Problem of Pain* (New York: Macmillan, 1962), pp. 40-41.

7. Charles Colson, "Making the World Safe for Religion," *Christianity Today*, November 8, 1993, p. 33.

8. David Hubbard, *The Holy Spirit in Today's World* (Waco, TX: Word, 1973), p. 29.

9. Robert Farrar Capon, *Between Noon and Three—A Parable of Romance, Law, and the Outrage of Grace* (San Francisco: Harper & Row, 1982), pp. 132-133.

10. J. R. R. Tolkien, *The Return of the King*, vol. 3 in *The Lord of the Rings* (New York: Ballantine, 1965), p. 283.

11. Helmut Thielicke, *Theological Ethics—Foundations*, William H. Lazareth, ed. (Grand Rapids: Eerdmans, 1979), p. 317.

12. Emil Brunner, *Truth as Encounter*, Loos and Cairns, trans. (Philadelphia: The Westminster Press, 1964), p. 117.

13. I am indebted to Doug Jackson for this story, which appeared in an unpublished manuscript he wrote and sent to me for review.

Eight—Community of Worship

1. As quoted by Elizabeth Achtemeier, "Cause for a Com-

mon Thanksgiving?" *Preaching*, November-December 1990, p. 14.

2. Brennan Manning, *Lion and Lamb—the Relentless Tenderness of Jesus* (Old Tappan, NJ: Chosen Books, 1986), pp. 96-97.

3. As told by Alan Jones, "Our Transubstantiation," *Pulpit Digest*, July/August 1993, p. 10.

4. As quoted by Richard Keyes, "The Idol Factory," *No God But God*, Os Guinness and John Seel, ed. (Chicago: Moody, 1992), p. 32.

5. As quoted in "Reflections," *Christianity Today*, October 21, 1988, p. 33.

6. As quoted by Paul Anderson, "Balancing Form and Freedom," *Leadership*, Spring 1986, p. 25.

7. As quoted by Eugene Peterson, *Reversed Thunder* (San Francisco: Harper & Row, 1988), p. 71.

8. Paul K. Jewett, *God, Creation, and Revelation—A Neo-Evangelical Theology* (Grand Rapids: Eerdmans, 1991), p. 192.

9. Annie Dillard, *Holy the Firm* (New York: Bantam, 1977), p. 60.

10. Kenneth Grahame, *The Wind in the Willows* (London: Methuen Children's Books Ltd, Magnet Reprint Edition, 1978), p. 135.

11. Ben Patterson, *The Grand Essentials* (Waco, TX: Word, 1987), p. 101.

12. Patterson, *The Grand Essentials*, p. 97.

Nine—Community of the Word

1. Neil Postman, *Technopoly* (New York: Knopf, 1992), p. 69.

2. Ted Koppel, as quoted in *Harpers*, January 1986.

3. As quoted by John Killinger, "You Are What You Believe," *Preaching*, July-August 1993, p. 27.

4. 1 Kings 19:11-12.

5. Psalm 33:6.

6. P. T. Forsyth, *The Person and Place of Christ* (London: Independent Press, 1909), p. 179.

7. James Patterson and Peter Kim, *The Day America Told the Truth—What People Really Believe About What Really*

Matters (New York: Plume, 1992).
8. Dale Bruner, *The Christbook* (Waco: Word, 1987), p. 305.
9. As told in *Parables, Etc.,* vol. 9, no. 9, November 1989, p. 6.
10. Romans 1:16.
11. James Daane, *Preaching With Confidence—A Theological Essay on the Power of the Pulpit* (Grand Rapids: Eerdmans, 1980), p. 27.
12. John Jess, "The Chapel of the Air," Radio Message 1123.
13. As quoted by Calvin Miller, *Spirit, Word, and Story: A Philosophy of Preaching* (Dallas: Word, 1989), p. 198.
14. F. Dale Bruner, "A Tale of Two Sons," *Christianity Today,* October 4, 1985, p. 47.
15. As told by John Hewitt, "To Illustrate . . ." *Leadership,* May-June 1993, p. 62.

Ten—Community of Love
1. Walter Eichrodt, *Theology of the Old Testament,* vol. I, J. A. Baker, trans. (London: SCM Press, 1961), p. 270.
2. Gerhard von Rad, *Old Testament Theology,* vol. I, D. M. G. Stalker, trans. (Edinburgh and London: Oliver & Boyd, 1962), p. 205.
3. George Marsden, *Reforming Fundamentalism* (Grand Rapids: Eerdmans, 1987), p. 7.
4. John Calvin, *Institutes of the Christian Religion,* vol. II, John T. McNeill, ed., Ford Lewis Battles, trans. (Philadelphia: Westminster, 1960), p. 1031.
5. Calvin, *Institutes of the Christian Religion,* vol. II, p. 1161.
6. John Macquarrie, *Principles of Christian Theology* (London: SCM Press, 1966), p. 343.
7. Macquarrie, *Principles of Christian Theology,* p. 343.
8. Macquarrie, *Principles of Christian Theology,* p. 364.
9. James Baldwin, as quoted by Robert A. Raines, *Creative Brooding* (New York: Macmillan, 1966), p. 48.
10. Karl Barth, *Church Dogmatics IV/2,* trans. G. W. Bromiley (Edinburgh: T. & T. Clark, 1958), p. 745.
11. Barth, *Church Dogmatics IV/2,* p. 787.
12. Barth, *Church Dogmatics IV/2,* p. 819.
13. Clyde Edgerton, *Walking Across Egypt* (New York: Ballantine, 1987), pp. 130-131.

14. Richard Selzer, *Mortal Lessons* (New York: Simon & Schuster, 1974), pp. 45-46.
15. Vachel Lindsay, from "General William Booth Enters into Heaven," in *The Mentor Book of Major American Poets*, ed. Oscar Williams and Edwin Honig (New York: New American Library, 1962), pp. 269-70.

Author

Donald Wayne McCullough is President and Professor of Theology and Preaching at San Francisco Theological Seminary. Previously, he was Pastor of Solana Beach Presbyterian Church in California for fourteen years and of Rainier Beach United Presbyterian Church in Seattle, Washington for four years.

Dr. McCullough received the Ph.D. in systematic theology from the University of Edinburgh, Scotland. He holds the M.Div. in theology from Fuller Theological Seminary and the B.A. in political science from Seattle Pacific University. As an adjunct professor, he has taught theology and homiletics at Fuller Theological Seminary and worship at San Francisco Theological Seminary. In addition to several books, he has published numerous journal and magazine articles especially in the areas of theology, ministry, literature, and the life of faith. He has also served in editorial capacities for *Christianity Today*; *Leadership Journal*; *Presbyterian Outlook*; and *Theology, News and Notes*.

Along with his keen interest in literature and the arts, Dr. McCullough is an avid sailor and runner. He and his wife, Karen, have two daughters, Jennifer and Joy.

Index of Names

Index of Scripture